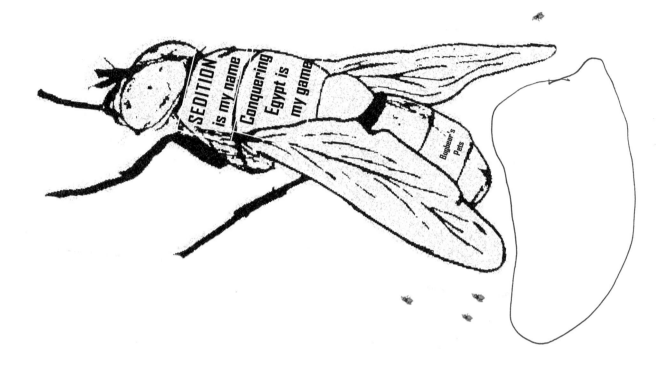

The 10 Plagues Placed On Egypt

Murdering Our Godhead

A Book of Witness

by

Angela Powell

This book is dedicated to you, the Redeemed, because you know the truth and are ready to be set free.

Convert to The Aten.

Thank you, Zavion and Cortez, just because you motivate me to fight for the freedoms of our little children. Because of you, The Aten Converter strives to print the truth in a format understandable to both young and old. I love you…But GOD Loves You More.

The Ba: Sent With A Grip

The Ba is the symbolic representation of your spirit and your soul. It takes the form of a small falcon with the head of a human being. Every essence of your unique personality is embodied

within your Ba. It gives you power and vitality. Via your Ba, you can fly up to God and spiritually interact with Him; and He with you *because even God has a Ba.* Your Ba even lives after death and rejoins with you to keep your vital mental and physical forces properly functioning.

I heard The Spirit say: "You Are Sent With A Grip."

God is using you

Meaning, you are a **Ba**, a human-headed falcon. ~~You are being~~ *as His falcon & train you* ~~trained~~ in falconry (Sent With A Grip) to scout out the Redeemed, save them, and bring them safely home to The Aten.

John 14:16 - 20

And I will pray the Father, and he shall give you another Comforter, that he may abide with you for ever; Even the Spirit of truth; whom the world cannot receive, because it seeth him not, neither knoweth him: but ye know him; for he dwelleth with you, and shall be in you. I will not leave you comfortless: I will come to you. Yet a little while, and the world seeth me no more; but ye see me: because I live, ye shall live also. At that day ye shall know that I am in my Father, and ye in me, and I in you (John 14:16 – 20).

Reading In Tongues and Translating

The New Beginning of Understanding the Ten Plagues Placed on Egypt

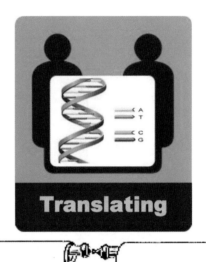

Translating

1John 4:4	1John 4:4
Ye are of God, **little children**, and have overcome them: because greater is he that is in you, than he that is in the world.	Ye are of God, **little *Atenites***, and have overcome *Shem and Japheth*: because greater is *The Aten* that is in you, *Ham*, than *Jehovah the God of mischief* that is in the *Western World*.

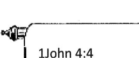

Contents

The Ba: Sent With A Grip .... Error! Bookmark not defined.

John 14:16 – 20, Another Comforter 5

Reading In Tongues and Translating 6

The Power Of Writing Down My Thoughts (Test Yourself Journaling Page) 9

The Lord God Alpha Khen Omega Speaks 11

Captive's Log 13

How To Use The Strong's Concordance 19

WORD STUDY: Jehovah = God of mischief 21

Captive's Log 22

Question: "Why Egypt?" 25

Captive's Log 26

The Cuckoo and the Warbler 29

WORD STUDY : Egypt = To Cause To Weigh That Which Causes Oppression and Anguish. 30

Pictographic Conclusion For "WHY EGYPT?" 32

JEHOVAH'S SPIRITUAL AGENDA 33

Revelation 19:9, An Invitation To The Marriage Supper of The Lamb 36

Question: "What is the intent of the 10 Plagues that Jehovah God of mischief Placed on Egypt?" 37

PLAGUE 1: WATER INTO BLOOD 39

Reading In Tongues and Translating 40

WORD STUDY: Blood = (English) bhel-[3] = To thrive, bloom, bless//(Hebrew) Death, Dumb 42

[handwritten: Small] *[handwritten: Smaller]*

Water = Mayim = To hear intelligently 43

Dry Land = Ashamed = To be disappointed 43

TODAY'S REVELATION: 44

PLAGUE 2: FROGS 45

Reading In Tongues and Translating .... Error! Bookmark not defined.

[handwritten: 46]

WORD STUDY: Frog = Furbish = Sword = To Depart Early 47

TODAY'S REVELATION: 48

PLAGUE 3: LICE FROM THE DUST OF THE EARTH 49

Reading In Tongues and Translating 50

WORD STUDY: Dust = Dove = Falcon = Vineyard of Christ 52

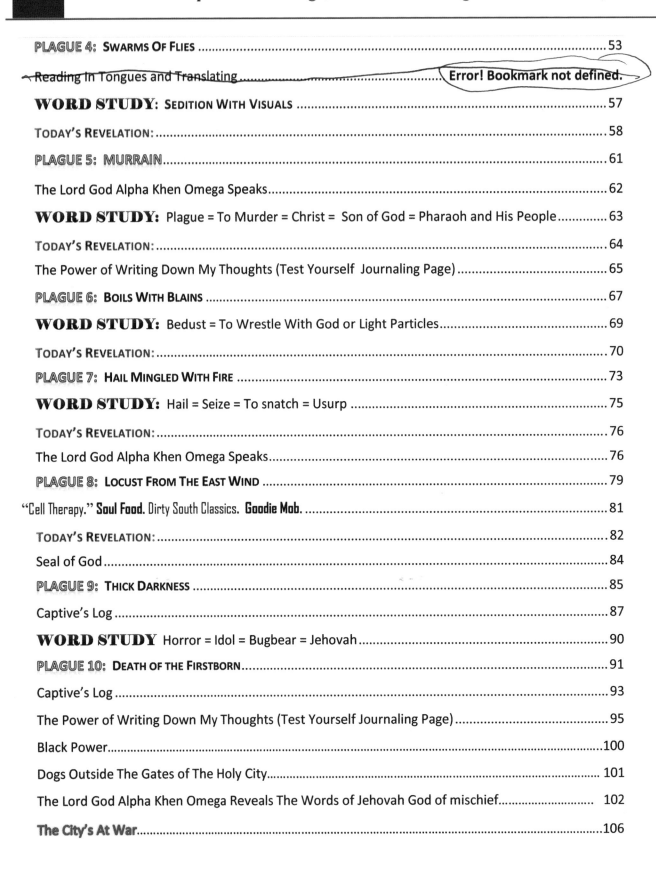

PLAGUE 4: SWARMS OF FLIES 53

Reading In Tongues and Translating .... Error! Bookmark not defined.

WORD STUDY: SEDITION WITH VISUALS 57

TODAY'S REVELATION: 58

PLAGUE 5: MURRAIN 61

The Lord God Alpha Khen Omega Speaks 62

WORD STUDY: Plague = To Murder = Christ = Son of God = Pharaoh and His People 63

TODAY'S REVELATION: 64

The Power of Writing Down My Thoughts (Test Yourself Journaling Page) 65

PLAGUE 6: BOILS WITH BLAINS 67

WORD STUDY: Bedust = To Wrestle With God or Light Particles 69

TODAY'S REVELATION: 70

PLAGUE 7: HAIL MINGLED WITH FIRE 73

WORD STUDY: Hail = Seize = To snatch = Usurp 75

TODAY'S REVELATION: 76

The Lord God Alpha Khen Omega Speaks 76

PLAGUE 8: LOCUST FROM THE EAST WIND 79

"Cell Therapy." Soul Food. Dirty South Classics. Goodie Mob. 81

TODAY'S REVELATION: 82

Seal of God 84

PLAGUE 9: THICK DARKNESS 85

Captive's Log 87

WORD STUDY Horror = Idol = Bugbear = Jehovah 90

PLAGUE 10: DEATH OF THE FIRSTBORN 91

Captive's Log 93

The Power of Writing Down My Thoughts (Test Yourself Journaling Page) 95

Black Power 100

Dogs Outside The Gates of The Holy City 101

The Lord God Alpha Khen Omega Reveals The Words of Jehovah God of mischief 102

The City's At War 106

The Power Of Writing Down My Thoughts

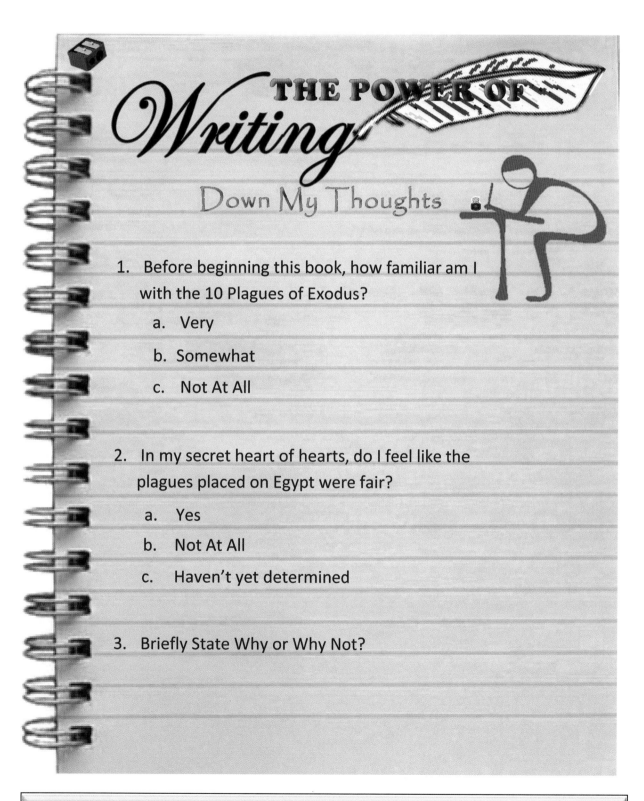

THE POWER OF Writing Down My Thoughts

1. Before beginning this book, how familiar am I with the 10 Plagues of Exodus?

    a. Very

    b. Somewhat

    c. Not At All

2. In my secret heart of hearts, do I feel like the plagues placed on Egypt were fair?

    a. Yes

    b. Not At All

    c. Haven't yet determined

3. Briefly State Why or Why Not?

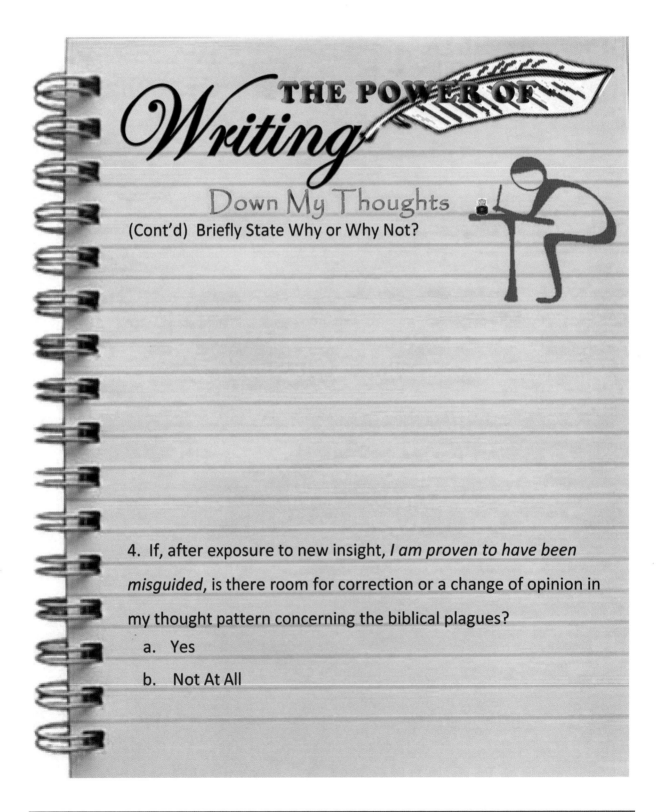

THE POWER OF
Writing
Down My Thoughts

(Cont'd) Briefly State Why or Why Not?

4. If, after exposure to new insight, *I am proven to have been misguided*, is there room for correction or a change of opinion in my thought pattern concerning the biblical plagues?

   a. Yes

   b. Not At All

The Lord God Alpha Khen Omega Speaks

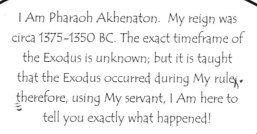

I Am Pharaoh Akhenaton. My reign was circa 1375-1350 BC. The exact timeframe of the Exodus is unknown; but it is taught that the Exodus occurred during My rule; therefore, using My servant, I Am here to tell you exactly what happened!

On various pages, I will jot down a few facts that I want you to keep in mind:

FACT 1

Pharaoh comes from the title "Sa Ra," which means "Son of God."

FACT 2

It is taught of the Egyptians that we worshipped many Gods. During My rule, there was only One God; Re-Harakhti-in-his-name-Shu-who is Aten.

I Am The Aten.

(Matthew 11:27)

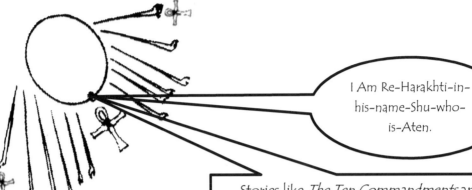

I Am Re-Harakhti-in-his-name-Shu-who-is-Aten.

Stories like *The Ten Commandments* and *Exodus: Gods and Kings* televise the war between Jehovah the God of mischief versus The Aten the Sun of Righteousness with healing in His wings. ⓘ

① You've seen it on TV via Jehovah's POV. Now, read about it from MY POV.

I Am The Son of The Aten. I and My Father are one.

I Am the God of the ancient Egyptian people. I Am also The Lord your God...*you just don't know it, yet.* My spiritual manifestation can cause **anguish**, I will, therefore, introduce this revelation with child-like innocence, to lessen the impact on your **medulla** oblongata. I will use a straightforward method of quoting Scripture verbatim and inserting English and or Hebrew definitions for key words appertaining to the 10 Plagues Placed On Egypt.

Place african map inside circle reading "covered in blood..."

Captive's Log

I am a servant of The Aten-in-His-new name-The Lord God AlphaKhenOmega. My ancestors were snatched, kidnapped and ~~enslaved in this land, which makes~~ me their *Western world.*

captive. The Aten has come to set me free ~~x~~ *from my kidnappers and oppressors.*

I am sitting here under extreme unction,

 *Bigger*

creating this book about the Exodus plagues, just for you, the Redeemed. As I let The Spirit of The Aten use me, I am learning along with you.

When you read about THE TEN PLAGUES in the Bible, during the initial reading, the magnitude of the catastrophes doesn't quite sink in. The 1st **Plague** turns water into blood, not only in Egypt but throughout all the African continental waterways.

Think about how far the Nile stretches from one end of African to the ~~next.~~ *other*

When you read about it, you are reading the passages so fast or listening to the preacher so intensely so that you can take notes, that your mind cannot yet conceive of what it looked like to see an entire landmass **covered in blood for 7 Days.** *Bigger*

Or even if you can phantom it, instead of shrieking in horror, you take sides, and say to your Christian-self, "The ancient Egyptians deserved what they got for enslaving the Hebrews/Israelites/Jews."

The whole purpose of these learning materials is to show you that you are the heir of the ancient Egyptians... your kingdom is usurped...

Abraham   Isaac   Jacob

... Usurpation In Progress...

Captive's Log

yOur people and you were and are enslaved by biblical patriarchs who practice the worst kinds of conjuration, sorcery, and witchcraft, casting spells over us so that they may permanently dominate us. You think these people are good, but they are very evil. The Bible calls them treacherous dealers ~~who~~ *that* dealt very treacherously (Isaiah 24:16).

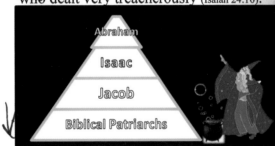

What have they done?

From Plague 1 to Plague 10,

Shemetic and Japhetic patriarchs cast spells that cause a state of dumbness-until-death throughout the African Continent so that the Hamitic people will never question the image of The Holy Ghost, *nor ponder other*

reasons for the death of The Christ

Our enemies depict The Holy Ghost as a white dove, disguised as a messenger of peace, waving a banner of love; all while they **besiege** us with hostilities and engage in clandestine warfare against Black peoples the world over.

The image of the real Holy Ghost is a dark-colored bird, which is described as the ancient Egyptian falcon. This truth has been stopped, and when you hear it, you become afraid. A word used to describe this "stoppage of truth" also means "To die" and "To deceive." They were informing you of their intent to murder the Son of God and His Holy Ghost; then, deceive you with the imitation that you faithfully buy into line, page, and biblical book.

Come, let us sit together and open the meaning of each plague by defining

Captive's Log

each word to see what they mean. For instance, in **Plague 2**, bringing "frogs" into "the land," is a camouflaged parable for saying a "furbished sword" is being sent throughout your continent.

This is not a novel; it is a pictographic book of definitions.

Come, engage in this word study with yOur God, and using yOur Holy Ghost Power…yOur Black Power, let us finally live up to the meaning of our name.

Do you know that *Egypt* means *anguish*, which comes from a root word meaning *"to cause to weigh ~~or consider~~ that which causes to oppress?"*

Once you find the root cause, you must of necessity do something to alleviate the oppression.

Do you even know that the biblical name for Egypt is Mizraim?

Mizraim means "BESIEGE PLACES."

Besiege comes from the word *"siege,"* which means *"throne," "falcon's nest,"* and to be *"created from one's self,"* which means you are ~~speaking about or~~ learning about The Egyptian origins of The Creator. ~~He is Lord God and~~ ^{stet} when you learn about YOUR Lord and His people, you must of necessity learn about **Ancestors of the same kind as you**.

Those definitions are from the tongues found in out-of-print books.

Using those books, I am going to condense the etymologies of several languages to give you in-depth definitions for what it means to be Hamitic seed from ancient Egypt suffering through THE TEN PLAGUES.

Captive's Log

yOur God is holy. His Word is excellent. His teaching is supreme. That is why as a Christian, you take pride in *speaking in tongues*. Now, the time has come when God wants you to take *speaking in tongues* one step further, and learn **Reading In Tongues.**

How do you do that?

AWESOME QUESTION!

Start with *The Strong's Hebrew/Greek Concordance;* the *Hieroglyphic Dictionary;* the 1968 Pokorny Etymology, which is affixed to the *American Heritage Dictionary;* and the 1877 *Gaelic Etymology of Western Europe.*

All of these languages shall combine and be to you during your studies like cloven tongues of fire sitting on you to make you understand that THE 10 PLAGUES PLACED ON EGYPT are long-term schemes aimed at murdering The Son of God and His Holy Ghost, then enslaving you.

Casted on Egypt circa 1375 BC, these plaques are what really caused The Crucifixion. Almost four thousand years later, these plagues are still active to this day to bring and keep everyone who is Black in bondage, and to destroy his culture, and to keep him from seeking his true Godhead.

PROVE IT TO YOURSELF!

Captive's Log

I want you to at least look up the name "JEHOVAH" in the Concordance.

Why should you?

What is the incentive?

If I could offer you a million dollars, I would…*just to incentivize you.*

But, I believe that you know there is something far greater than money!

Think in terms of Mark 13:22 and Revelation 12:9. Those two verses tell you that "the whole world is deceived, except The Elect." That means no matter how often you sit in church under your pastor's tutelage, no matter how often you pay tithes, no matter your baptism, no matter how many times a day you call on the name, "Jesus Christ," **you are deceived**…*unless you are an ELECT.*

Of course you are going to say, "I am not deceived, therefore I am accounted as the very elect."

I will not and cannot dispute your assurance in God, *if you take this one test for yourself:*

LOOK up the name of Jehovah.

Do not postpone it…**Do it RIGHT NOW!**

Here, I will help you.

I realize not everyone has access to a Bible Concordance. In fact, some of you may not even know what it is. That is okay. At one point, neither did I! God showed it to me in a vision in my head upon my bed. I thought I was special, but after years of learning, I now know that what God taught me was not just for me alone, but for you as well.

Captive's Log

I will tell you about *Strong's Hebrew and Greek Concordance*. It is a foreign language dictionary. You SEE, the Bible was originally written in Hebrew, Aramaic, and Greek. We, now, have it in modern English. For serious studying, at some point, you have to revisit the original texts, which is why The Spirit of God is saying to you: That you need to **read in tongue**.

You need to see the Hebrew, Aramaic, and Greeks lexicons in order to be gifted with a CROWN OF LEARNING that guarantees your spiritual election, and ensures that you do not fall victim to deceptions (Revelation 3:11).

Using a hardbound concordance is great, but I have uncovered the scholar's secret—The Concordance on CD-Rom.

I am excited to show it to you.

My plan is to use my Screen Capture to take snapshots of what a concordance looks like, so that you may SEE *"read"* the foreign tongues.

We are going to start with the name "JEHOVAH."

Page 11 of 12

Page 12 of 12

How To Use The Strong's Concordance

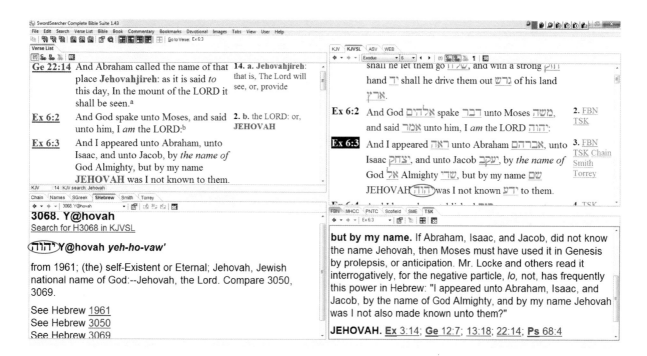

INSTRUCTIONS:

➢ This is an image on my computer screen. I will paste it at the beginning of each "Plague" chapter.

➢ It is displaying *The Sword Searchers* program on CD-Rom.

➢ To use the program, I type the name "Jehovah," in the program's "Search" box.

➢ As you can see, every Scripture with the name "Jehovah" displays in Box 1, the first box, top left.

- ○ I chose Exodus 6:3, the Scripture where God tells Abraham that the ancient people did not know him by the name of JEHOVAH. (Jehovah came later, in your timeframe, circa AD 1530-1611.)

- ➤ Next, I move on to Box 2, the box located top right.

  - o It displays the actual verse Exodus 6:3.

  - o The green underlined characters are Hebrew words that come from *Strong's Concordance*, which is linked to *Sword Searchers* KJV Bible.

  - o The KJV Bible only uses the actual name "Jehovah" a total of seven times. When referencing God, the KJV uses the terms "God," "Lord," and "Lord God."

  - o When I hover my mouse on the green character for Jehovah, the definition displays in Box 3.

- ➤ In Box 3, lower left, the Hebraic definition for the name "Jehovah" displays. It is assigned the number H3068.

- ➤ Box 4, lower right, displays all commentaries associated with the biblical verse.

- ➤ Back to Box 3. All Hebrew, Aramaic, and Greek words are assigned a number.

  - o The number for "JEHOVAH," H3068, reads that it comes from the number H1961. So you are supposed to go to the "Search" box and type in H1961. This will display the root word for the name Jehovah. It will also tell you which action to take next.

    - ▪ The definition for the name "Jehovah," which is number H3068, Y@hovah, reads: From 1961; (the) self-Existent or Eternal; Jehovah, Jewish national name of God:--Jehovah, the Lord. Compare 3050, 3069.

    - ▪ The definition for H1961 reads: A primitive root (compare 1933); to exist, i.e. be or become, come to pass (always emphatic, and not a mere copula or auxiliary):--beacon, X altogether, be(-come), accomplished, committed, like), break, cause, come (to pass), do, faint, fall, + follow, happen, X have, last, pertain, quit (one-)self, require, X use. See Hebrew 1933.

- To shorten the process, once you go through all the instructions and follow all the links to see this number or that number you end up with a chart that should look like this:

WORD STUDY

Jehovah = God of mischief

Jehovah	Jah + hovah = God of mischief
H3068. Y@hovah - from 1961; (the) self-Existent or Eternal; Jehovah, Jewish national name of God:-Jehovah, the Lord. See Hebrew 1961; See Hebrew 3050; See Hebrew 3069	H3050. Yahh - contraction for **3068**, and meaning the same; Jah, the sacred name: -- **Jah**, the Lord, most vehement. See Hebrew 3068
H1961. hayah - a primitive root; to exist, i.e. be or become, come to pass. See Hebrew 1933	+
H1933. hava'- a primitive root; **to breathe**. See Hebrew 183; See Hebrew 1961	H1943. **hovah** - another form for 1942; ruin:-- **mischief**
H183. 'avah - a primitive root; to wish for:--covet	H1942. havvah- **from 1933** (in the sense of eagerly coveting and rushing upon; by implication, of falling); desire; also ruin:--calamity, iniquity, **mischief**, mischievous (thing), naughtine ss, noisome, perverse thing, substance, **very wickedness**. See Hebrew 1933.
H3050. Yahh - contraction for **3068**, and meaning the same; Jah, the sacred name:-Jah, the Lord, most vehement. See Hebrew 3068	**H1933.** hava' - a primitive root; **To Breath**. See Hebrew 183; See Hebrew 1961
	"To Breath" = Terah, the father of Abraham

Taken from *Strong's Hebrew/Greek Concordance*

Captive's Log

Take a few minutes...

LOOK and SEE this graph and those that shall follow. Just stare at them until all those mind-consuming definitions in these two charts and the upcoming charts dress your mind in a new mental picture. The picture is the most important piece of wedding garment that God is going to give you to prepare for the "Marriage Supper of the Lamb (Revelation 19:7-9)."

What is this mental garment?

Can you see it?

"...JEHOVAH..."

It comes from two words: "Jah," which means "GOD, THE LORD MOST VEHEMENT;" and "hovah," which means "MISCHIEF."

Combined, the definitions for "Jehovah" mean "God of mischief."

Jehovah has presented himself to you as a holy Father-God; but he has done nothing but evil to the Black man. By writing THE 10 PLAGUES PLACED ON EGYPT, I hope to show you exactly what Jehovah has done, courtesy of The Lord God Alpha Khen Omega.

Make Sure To Cross Reference With **SPIRITUAL BIPOLAR: GOD IS THE PEACE IN YOUR HEART THAT CALMS THE VOICES ABOVE YOUR HEAD.**

Page 22

Captive's Log

That is very frightening information!

Not only frightening—it causes destabilization!

You are now dressed up for a MARRIAGE SUPPER two thousand years in the making; only to learn that you believe in a God of mischief who deceives everybody in the whole wide world…except the very elect.

Page 3 of 4

If you can SEE and understand the definitions, you are now an ELECT. And, you have a dozen questions. I have anticipated what they are and will answer them by-and-by within this study.

Page 4 of 4

Make Sure To Cross Reference With **SPIRITUAL BIPOLAR: GOD IS THE PEACE IN YOUR HEART THAT CALMS THE VOICES ABOVE YOUR HEAD.**

Page 24

Biblical References:

Behold the land of the Chaldeans (Abraham, Place of Occult): this people was not, till the Assyrian founded it for them that dwell in the wilderness: they set up the towers thereof, they raised up the palaces thereof; and he brought it to ruin (Isaiah 23:13).

For thus saith the Lord GOD, My people went down aforetime into Egypt to sojourn there; and the Assyrian oppressed them without cause (Isaiah 52:4).

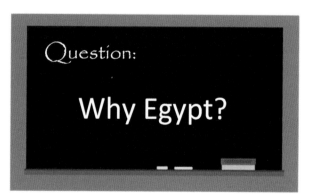

Question:

Why Egypt?

Captive's Log

Question: "Why Egypt?"

Answer: "Isaiah 23:13 and 52:4."

Before we begin our breakdown of each plague, I want you to consider Isaiah 23:13 and 52:4. Summarized, it tells you that the **Assyrians** and **Chaldeans are one people** and that they are the people **who usurp the kingdom** of Egypt and hold the Egyptians and Canaanites in bondage. You know how the religious sect teaches that the Egyptians held the Hebrews and Israelites in bondage—well, forget about that!

Shemetic and Japhetic heirs teach a doctrine that is vice versa to the how the Scriptures teach it. A careful eye can hone in on the truth. Chaldeans are from Ur of the Chaldees. Ur of the Chaldees is the place of the occults.

Ur is Abraham's homeland. Abraham's name means "Naked; Strong Thief." Everything these patriarchs did to Egypt was evil from the beginning!

THE TEN PLAGUES placed on Egypt did not start with Moses. They started with Abraham, Isaac, Jacob, and Joseph; and even Noah, Shem and Terah; and Japheth and Magog, from whence shall come the War of Gog and Magog, They operate under the authority of the Godhead of all White men.

Abraham's forefathers lived well into their 900th years. They were the reincarnated spirit-guides of Abraham, Isaac, and Jacob, and yes, even Joseph and Moses.

Come on! Think about it!

Captive's Log

Noah did not die until he was 950 YEARS OLD. **Shem** did not die until he was 600 YEARS OLD. **Terah** did not die until he was 205 YEARS OLD.

They had a 1000-years to implement

A SPIRITUAL AGENDA

conducive to murdering The Son of God and His Holy Ghost and to enslaving His people!

Proof is in the definitions of their names...

 it out sometimes.

Why did Noah, Shem and Japheth (Jews and Greeks) choose to plague Egypt?

Why not the ancient civilizations of Jericho or Sumer?

I will tell you why Egypt!

Egypt means "ANGUISH" and "OPPRESSION." As an Egyptian, you will be the first to sense the yoke of bondage approaching, and you will be the first to rise up and fight against oppression. Your **ENEMY IS AN OPPRESSOR**; his job is to cause you to feel oppression. He wants to STOP you before you rise up to STOP him from oppressing and enslaving yOur peoples a third time!

The Oppressor's Credo is: If I, The Devil, can murder "The Sa Ra" and enslave His peoples...well then, the world and the cattle upon a thousand hills are mine to do with as I please!

Captive's Log

Because of your loyalty to foreign Gods of mischief and his oppressing heirs, some of you have "Confusion of Face (Daniel 9:8)" and do not know who you truly are. You are Egyptians…the biblical Hamites. The confusion makes it difficult for you to call upon the name of The Aten. You are accustomed to calling on the name of Jesus Christ. That is okay! Just remember Jesus Christ is The Son of God. The term "Son of God" comes from the ancient title "Sa Ra," which means "Pharaoh, Son of God."

Historically, physically, and spiritually, Egypt is the sure cornerstone. Her architects have far outlasted all ancient structures of the world. Jehovah the God of mischief schemes to implant his seed in the great pyramids in order to oppress and murder the aboriginals (Redeemed), *much like a cuckoo plants her eggs inside the nest of a reed warbler.*

Of course you know how that story ends—the cuckoo kills the warbler chicks and the warbler parents rear the cuckoos instead of her own young. Egypt is now rearing cuckoos and one-by-one Jehovah's heirs are enslaving, oppressing, and murdering us, the true native Egyptians.

Not only are they our Oppressors; they are the crème de la crème of our "Accusers." They enslave us but turn the tables to accuse us of historically brutalizing them. They are such hard-hitting Satanic accusers, that they make us hate ourselves for crimes and sins that we never committed against them or their gods.

Page 5 of 6   Page 6 of 6

The Cuckoo and the Warbler

I am a Cuckoo; a brood parasite. I lay my eggs in the warbler's nest. My son kills the warbler's chicks and takes the place of her young. My son takes and takes from the warbler and gives nothing in return.

Reed warbler feeding a cuckoo chick that cannot even fit into the nest.

"WHAT HAVE YOU DONE WITH MY BABIES, YOU FAKE WARBLER!"

"ONCE MY CHILDREN REALIZE HOW JEHOVAH THE GOD OF MISCHIEF TRICKS THEM, OPPRESSES THEM, AND KILLS THEM, THEY WILL RISE UP TO TAKE BACK THEIR ANCESTRAL NEST."

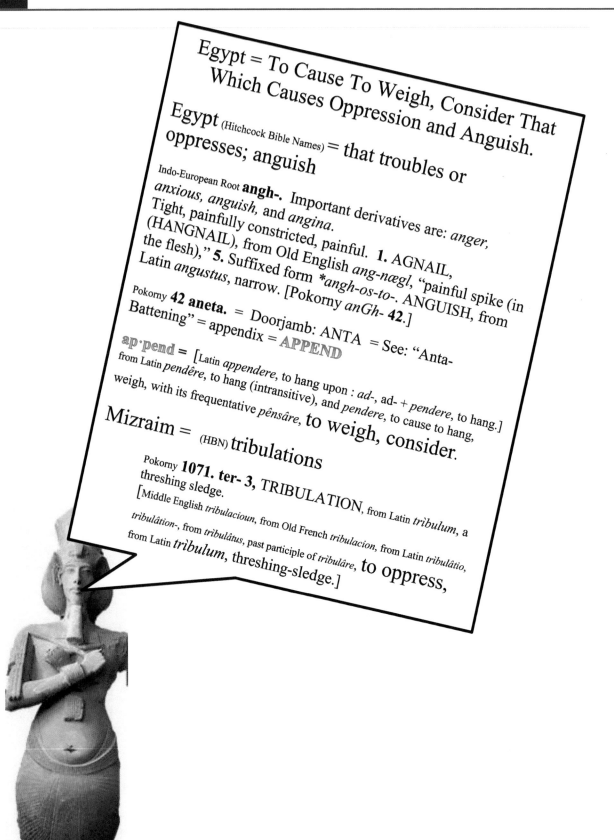

Egypt = To Cause To Weigh, Consider That Which Causes Oppression and Anguish.

Egypt (Hitchcock Bible Names) = that troubles or oppresses; anguish

Indo-European Root **angh-.** Important derivatives are: *anger, anxious, anguish,* and *angina.* Tight, painfully constricted, painful. **1.** AGNAIL, (HANGNAIL), from Old English *ang-nægl,* "painful spike (in the flesh)," **5.** Suffixed form **angh-os-to-.* ANGUISH, from Latin *angustus,* narrow. [Pokorny *anGh-* **42.**]

Pokorny **42 aneta.** = Doorjamb: ANTA = See: "Anta-Battening" = appendix = APPEND

ap·pend = [Latin *appendere,* to hang upon : *ad-,* ad- + *pendere,* to hang.] from Latin *pendêre,* to hang (intransitive), and *pendere,* to cause to hang, weigh, with its frequentative *pênsâre,* to weigh, consider.

Mizraim = (HBN) tribulations

Pokorny **1071. ter- 3,** TRIBULATION, from Latin *tribulum,* a threshing sledge. [Middle English *tribulacioun,* from Old French *tribulacion,* from Latin *tribulâtio, tribulâtion-,* from *tribulâtus,* past participle of *tribulâre,* to oppress, from Latin *tribulum,* threshing-sledge.]

WORD STUDY

4714. Mitsrayim = dual of 4693; Mitsrajim, i.e. Upper and Lower Egypt:-- Egypt, Egyptians, Mizraim.

See Hebrew 4693

4693. matsowr = the same as 4692 in the sense of a limit; Egypt (as the border of Palestine):--BESIEGED PLACES, defense, fortified.

BE·SIEGED

[Middle English *besegen*, probably (with substitution of *bi-*, be-), from *assegen*, from Old French *assegier*, from Vulgar Latin **assedicâre* : Latin *ad-*, **ad-** + Vulgar Latin ***sedicâre*, to sit** (from Latin *sedêre*). See **siege**.]

siege (sêj) *noun* = **3.** *Obsolete.* A seat, especially a throne.

[Middle English *sege*, from Old French, seat, from Vulgar Latin **sedicum*, from **sedicâre*, to sit, from Latin *sedêre*.]

Pokorny 884. sed- = To sit//Throne, seat, SOIL(1)//See: **nizdo-**

Pokorny 884. ked- = To go, yield

Pokorny 887. **nizdo-** = Bird's nest//"place where the bird sits down."//

NIDIFY, EYAS// **ey·as** = A nestling hawk or **falcon**, especially one to be trained for falconry.

[Middle English *eias*, from *an eias*, alteration of **a nias*, an eyas, from Old French *niais*, from Latin *nìdus*, nest.]
nid·i·fy (nîd¹e-fî´) *verb, intransitive*

nid·i·fied, nid·i·fy·ing, nid·i·fies = **To build a nest.**

Indo-European Root

Pokorny 235. dhē- = Important derivatives are: *do¹*, *deed*, *doom*, *-dom*,

deem, fact, factor, fashion, feat¹, feature, affair, affect¹, affection, amplify, benefit, defeat,

defect, effect, efficient, infect, justify, modify, notify, perfect, profit, qualify, sacrifice, face,

surface, difficulty, thesis, and *theme.*

To set, put. Contracted from **dheə-*. **1.** O-grade form **dhō-*. DO¹; FORDO, from Old English *dōn*, to do, from Germanic **dōn*. **2.** Suffixed form **dhē-ti-*, "thing laid down or done, law, deed." DEED, from Old English *dǣd*, doing, deed, from Germanic **dēdiz*. **3.** Suffixed o-grade form **dhō-mo-*. **a.** DOOM, from Old English *dōm*, judgment (< "thing set or put down") **(NIDIFY)**, to do, make, and Latin combining form *-fex* (< **-fak-s*), "maker"; **b.** FAÇADE, FACE, (FACET), (FACIAL), FACIES; (DEFACE), EFFACE, (SURFACE), from Latin derivative *faciēs*, shape, face (< "form imposed on something"); **14.** Suffixed form **dhē-to-*, set down, created.

(see **s(w)e-**) Old Iranian compound **khvatō-dāta-*, **created from oneself**. [Pokorny 2. *dhē-* 235.]

created from oneself = 882, s(w)e-//Lord

882, swo-//Of the same kind

Pictographic Conclusion For "WHY EGYPT?"

Holy Ghost

place where the Bird Sits down

Aten, Sun/Son of God

I am a Bird

Make Sure To Cross Reference With **SPIRITUAL BIPOLAR: GOD IS THE PEACE IN YOUR HEART THAT CALMS THE VOICES ABOVE YOUR HEAD.**

Page 34

Make Sure To Cross Reference With **SPIRITUAL BIPOLAR: GOD IS THE PEACE IN YOUR HEART THAT CALMS THE VOICES ABOVE YOUR HEAD.**

Page 36

Question:

What is the intent of the 10 Plagues that Jehovah the God of mischief Placed on Egypt?

Answer: Exodus 4:22 – 23

And thou Moses (= to draw out, exegesis, create an excerpt) shalt say unto Pharaoh (Son of God), Thus saith the LORD (Jehovah the God of mischief), Israel is my son, even my firstborn: And I say unto thee, Let my son go, that he may serve me: and if thou refuse to let him go, behold, I will slay thy son, even thy firstborn.

(He will rule as God)

The death of the firstborn doesn't happen until the very last plague in Exodus 12:12; but as you can see from verse 4:22, Jehovah's heart is intent on murdering Egypt's firstborn, even The Son of God. To prove My point, starting with Plague 1 all the way to Plague 10, I will list each Scripture, and insert definitions for the wordsmith's chosen words appertaining to the plagues. Think of the scriptural verses as **"reading in the tongue"** and the inserted definitions as **"the translation."**

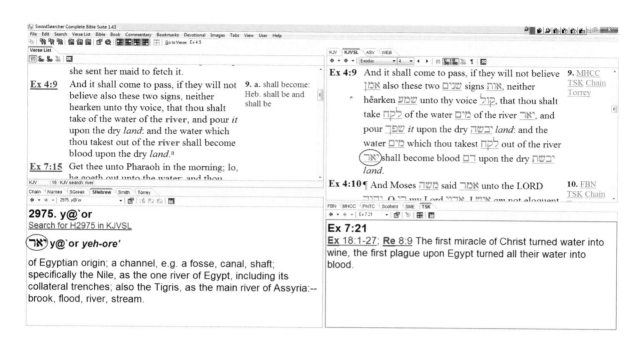

she sent her maid to fetch it.

Ex 4:9 And it shall come to pass, if they will not believe also these two signs, neither hearken unto thy voice, that thou shalt take of the water of the **river**, and pour *it* upon the dry *land*: and the water which thou takest out of the **river** shall become blood upon the dry *land*.ᵃ

9. a. shall become: Heb. shall be and shall be

Ex 7:15 Get thee unto Pharaoh in the morning; lo, he goeth out unto the water; and thou

2975. y@`or
Search for H2975 in KJVSL

y@`or *yeh-ore'*

of Egyptian origin; a channel, e.g. a fosse, canal, shaft; specifically the Nile, as the one river of Egypt, including its collateral trenches; also the Tigris, as the main river of Assyria:-- brook, flood, river, stream.

Ex 4:9 And it shall come to pass, if they will not believe אָמַן also these two שְׁנַיִם signs אוֹת, neither hearken שָׁמַע unto thy voice קוֹל, that thou shalt take לָקַח of the water מַיִם of the river יְאֹר, and pour שָׁפַךְ *it* upon the dry יַבָּשָׁה *land*: and the water מַיִם which thou takest לָקַח out of the river יְאֹר shall become blood דָּם upon the dry יַבָּשָׁה *land*.

9. MHCC TSK Chain Torrey

Ex 4:10 ¶ And Moses מֹשֶׁה said אָמַר unto the LORD

10. FBN TSK Chain

Ex 7:21
Ex 18:1-27; Re 8:9 The first miracle of Christ turned water into wine, the first plague upon Egypt turned all their water into blood.

Plague 1: Water Into Blood

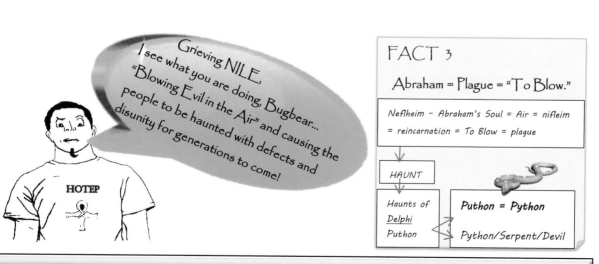

Grieving NILE, I see what you are doing, Bugbear... "Blowing Evil in the Air" and causing the people to be haunted with defects and disunity for generations to come!

HOTEP

FACT 3

Abraham = Plague = "To Blow."

Neflheim – Abraham's Soul = Air = nifleim = reincarnation = To Blow = plague

HAUNT

Haunts of Delphi Puthon

Puthon = Python

Python/Serpent/Devil

Turning water into blood is a spell that causes dumbness-until-death ~~and~~ throughout the African Continent by:

✓ Killing Black Unity
✓ Causing one to severely grieve
✓ Casting a lot for rulership in your enemies' favor
✓ Stoppage of truth/maā-t
✓ Inability to produce pure, clean, holy children
✓ Your enemies shall thrive and bloom while you perish

Come; let us *Read In Tongues* and have a closer look at the Scriptures with their definitions...

Reading In Tongues and Translating

Exodus 4:9 and 7:19   Water Into Blood

And it shall come to pass, if they will not believe also these two signs, neither hearken unto thy voice, that thou shalt take of the water *(mayim)* of the river *(Nile {the Gaelic Etymology states the definition for Africa is "the country of the flowing River, the Nile," pg. 565)*, and pour it upon the dry land *(to be ashamed, disappointed, or confused)* and the water which thou takest out of the river shall become blood *((Hebrew) to be dumb as if in death//(English) to thrive, bloom, bless)* upon the dry land *(to be ashamed, disappointed, or confused from waiting upon a successor, a sovereign, a Lord, a Son of God/Pharaoh who looks like you to come but who does not come in his appointed time)* (Exodus 4:9)

Make Sure To Cross Reference With **SPIRITUAL BIPOLAR: GOD IS THE PEACE IN YOUR HEART THAT CALMS THE VOICES ABOVE YOUR HEAD.**

Page 40

(Teacher)

And the LORD spake unto Moses, Say unto Aaron, Take thy rod, and stretch out thine hand upon the waters *(mayim*, heaven; place of intelligent hearing*)* of Egypt (anguish; place that weighs that which causes oppression), upon their streams, (5102. Nahar = a primitive root; to sparkle, i.e. (figuratively) be cheerful; hence (from the sheen of a running stream) to flow, i.e. (figuratively) assemble:--flow (together), be lightened {specifically, by pouring blood onto this assembly, it means to interrupt Black unity})

upon their rivers, (2975. y@˘or. //fosse/fossa/bone/dig {specifically, the meaning of pouring blood into the River Nile is to dry up the strength of African divinity, even to the bones of the Ancient of Days})

and upon their ponds, (98. 'agam//5701. ˘agam = a primitive root; to be sad:--cause to grieve)

and upon all their pools of water, (6960. Qavah = a primitive root//6957. qav = from 6960 (compare 6961); a cord (as connecting), especially for measuring; figuratively, a rule; also a rim, a musical string or accord:--line. Compare 6978.//cord = a lot//cast a lot to rule) that they may become blood; and that there may be blood (death and dumbness) throughout all the land of Egypt, both in vessels of wood, (stoppage of Truth/Maā-t) and in vessels of stone (stoppage of a builder, obtain children//Goddess, produce, create pure, clean boy or girl (Exodus 7:19)).

WORD STUDY
Blood = bhel-^{3} = To thrive, bloom, bless

Blood
Indo-European Root

bhel-^{3}. Important derivatives are: *foliage, folio, bloom^1, blossom, flora, flour, flourish, flower, bleed, blood, bless,* and *blade.*

To thrive, bloom. Possibly from **bhel-^{2}**.

I. Suffixed o-grade form **bhol-yo-,* leaf.

II. Extended form **bhlê-* (< **bhlee-*). **1. a.** BLOW^3, **b.** (*i*) BLOOM^1, BLOOM^2, from Old English *bloma,* a hammered ingot of iron (semantic development obscure). **c.** BLOSSOM, **d.** FERRET^2, **e.** suffixed form *bhlo-to-*; (*i*) BLEED, BLOOD, from Old English *blod,* blood; (*ii*) BLESS, from Old English *bloedsian, blêtsian,* to consecrate, from Germanic **blodison,* to treat or hallow with blood... etc... [Pokorny 4. *bhel-* 122.] {NOTE: This definition is not found in the 1968-69 version of AHD, it is only located in the 1995-96 CD-Rom version.} [Pokorny 4. *bhel-* 122.]

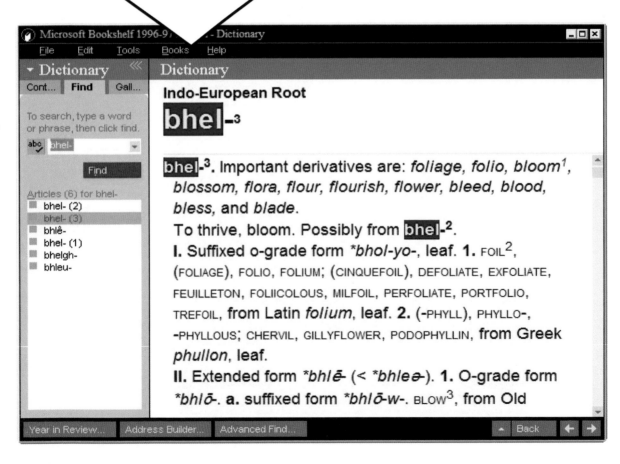

WORD STUDY
Water = Mayim = To hear intelligently

H4325. mayim = dual of a primitive noun (but used in a singular sense); water; figuratively, juice; by euphemism, urine, semen:--+ piss, wasting, water(-ing, (-course, -flood, -spring)).

Corresponding etymons:

H8064. shamayim =:--air, X astrologer, heaven(-s).

H8085. shama`= a primitive root; to hear intelligently:

Blood = Death = To be dumb

Blood = Dam = To be dumb, have death (Hebrew)
Blood = bhel-[3] = To thrive, bloom, bless (English)

H1818. dam = from 1826, blood (as that which when shed causes death) of man or an animal; + innocent.

H1826. damam = a prim root (compare 1724, 1820); to be dumb; by implication, to be astonished, to stop; also to perish:--cease, be cut down (off), forbear, hold peace, quiet self, rest, be silent, keep (put to) silence, be (stand) still, tarry, wait.

See Hebrew 1724. See Hebrew 1820. See Hebrew 1826.
See Hebrew 119.

Dry Land = Ashamed = To be disappointed

Dry Land = Yabbashah/Yabesh = To be ashamed

H3004. yabbashah = from 3001; dry ground:--dry (ground, land).

H3001. yabesh = a primitive root; to be ashamed, confused or disappointed; also (as failing) to dry up (as water) or wither (as herbage):--be ashamed, clean, be confounded, (make) dry (up), (do) shame(-fully), X utterly, wither (away).

TODAY'S REVELATION:

"Moses" was chosen because his name means "drawn forth." "Drawn forth" comes from the word "To draw." Its etymon is "tragh-," which means "to extract a literary passage; write an excerpt (Pokorny #1089)." Anyone who can excerpt Egypt's ancient texts for good or evil purposes is a type of Moses. Moses and Jehovah the God of mischief used Egypt's texts to cast a long-lasting spell effectively causing you to be ashamed and disappointed in Me, The Aten. This spell causes you to have CONFUSION OF FACE (Daniel 9:8) because you are waiting for an African successor or sovereign Lord, Who looks like you, to come; but Who doesn't appear in His appointed season. Therefore, you accept an alien Son of God whose lot is cast to rule in place of the true Son of God. This overthrow causes death and dumbness throughout your continent. It casts truth/maā-t to the ground (Daniel 8:12), and it kills Black unity so that as a people we can never get on One Accord with The Spirit of our ancestral Godhead.

There is a true Christ and there is an Anti-Christ, which means anti-Black. yOur African fountainhead is even **RIGHT NOW** under attack and you are still drinking the cursed blood of the Antichrist in place of yOur living waters, which gushes forth from Me, The Son of God/Sa Ra/Pharaoh. The etymons for "water" are the same as those for "heaven" and "to hear intelligently." The information you are to hear intelligently can be found on My YouTube Channel @ AlphaKhenOmega News.

Now that a plaguing spell has been cast, what pestilence will follow Jehovah's conjuration to bring about the death of the true Son of God/Pharaoh and cause a state of dumbness over the seed of Ham?

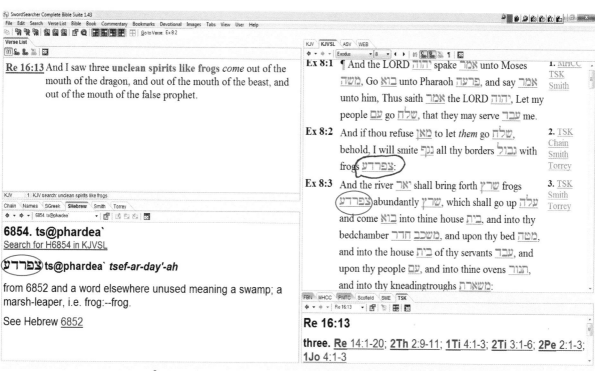

Reading In Tongues and Translating

Summoning forth frogs from the River Nile is a spell that brings a "furbished sword" throughout your continent to destroy the people and everything in your country's storehouses. Your storehouses include:

✓ Anything causing you to have light, fire, warmth, especially your mind
✓ Your continental currency, money supply
✓ A ruling government
✓ Food production
✓ Military Power

Come; let us *Read In Tongues* and have a closer look at the Scriptures with their definitions…

Exodus 8:1 – 4 Frogs From The Nile River

And the LORD (Jehovah the God of mischief) spake unto Moses (make an excerpt of Authoritative texts to gain an understanding of how to stand before God and act on His behalf), Go unto Pharaoh (The Son of God), and say unto him, Thus saith the LORD, Let my people go, that they may serve me. And if thou refuse to let them go, behold, I will smite all thy borders with frogs: And the river shall bring forth frogs ((English) Furbish, sword, leaping with joy; (Hebrew) H6852, Depart early) abundantly, which shall go up and come into thine house, and into thy bedchamber, and upon thy bed, (these three are equivalent to saying your Continent, your country, your state, to find your apartment and your very own bed) and into the house of thy servants, and upon thy people, and into thine ovens (H8574 tannuwr, light, fire, mind), and into thy kneadingtroughs (H4863, mish'ereth, your storehouses): And the frogs shall come up both on thee, and upon thy people, and upon all thy servants.

WORD STUDY

Frog = Furbish = Sword = To Depart Early

(Pokorny 845) preu-. = To hop. 1. (Old English) FROG. 2. (Middle Dutch) vro, "leaping with joy," happy: FROLIC.

(Pokorny 845) prep- = To appear. (Germanic) *furbjan, to cause to have a (good) appearance, polish, burnish: FURBISH

Pokorny # 845 is only found in the hard edition not the CD-Rom.

Notes:

{No search result in Concordance or Scriptures for the word "Frolic."}

{Furbish is the biblical adjective for "sword."}

Taken from *American Heritage Dictionary*.

Frog = Depart Early

6854. ts@phardea` = from 6852 and a word elsewhere unused meaning a swamp; a marsh-leaper, i.e. frog:--frog.

See Hebrew 6852.

H6852. tsaphar = a primitive root; to skip about, i.e. return:--**depart early**.

Supporting Scripture for "**DEPART EARLY**" is Judges 7:3

Taken from *Strong's Hebrew/Greek Concordance*.

TODAY'S REVELATION:

> **Judges 7:3**
> Now therefore go to, proclaim in the ears of the people, saying, Whosoever is fearful and afraid, let him return and **depart early** from mount **Gilead**. And there returned of the people twenty and two thousand; and there remained ten thousand.

"Gilead" comes from two Hebrew etymons meaning "heap" and "stone of testimony." So the message to you today is:

"When you hear this testimony, if you are fearful and afraid to war against Jehovah the God of mischief, against Abraham, Isaac, Jacob, and Joseph, then DEPART EARLY and return to them and be like Jehovah's unclean spirits like frogs leaping with joy upon the Egyptians to oppress them."

As an Egyptian, the definition mandates that you recognize who or what causes oppression and that you fight to overcome that obstacle or that you succumb to that obstacle. The plague of frogs releases a "furbished sword." Either you are a sword (spiritually, mentally, and physically) in My army, the army of The Aten; or you are a sword in the army of Jehovah the God of mischief.

Once the furbished sword is released, to bring about the death of The Son of God/Pharaoh and cause dumbness throughout the African Continent, what plagues will the God of mischief conjure up next to ignite his schemes?

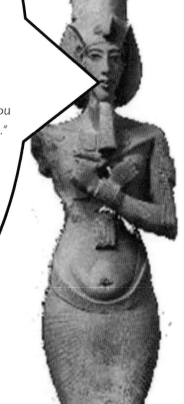

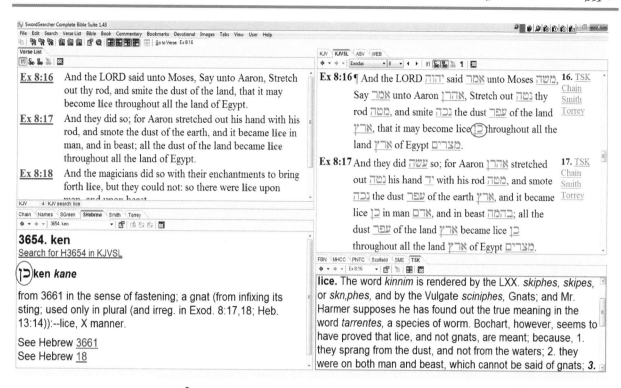

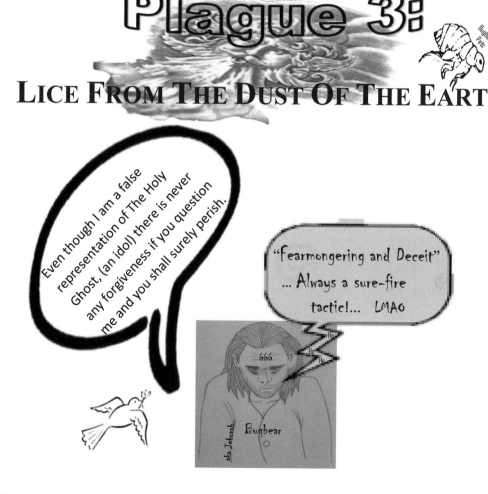

Plague 3:

LICE FROM THE DUST OF THE EARTH

Jehovah the God of mischief casts a Death Spell on all the firstborn sons of Ham. He then conjures up a furbished sword to go forth to kill them; but he especially has in his mind to kill The Son of God/Pharaoh and His Holy Ghost by sending a plague of lice into the Hamitic vineyard. The camouflaged word for **LICE** is **MANGER**. The attack is on The Son of God, even before He is born in the earth. How will Jehovah do it?

- ✓ Feed you a misrepresentation of the "Dove"
- ✓ Try to make the representation of the real "Dove" disappear or die
- ✓ Make you buy into the deceit
- ✓ Make you afraid to question his misrepresentations
- ✓ Blind your eyes so that you cannot Watch for the vineyard where the MANGER grows
- ✓ The MANGER is the birth-bed of Christ
- ✓ Curse Christ's MANGER, and cause you to rebel against YOUR native Godhead
- ✓ Murder and rub away all traces of those who know the truth about Jehovah the God of mischief
- ✓ Subdue the rest of the people of God

Come; let us *Read In Tongues* and have a closer look at the Scriptures with their definitions...

Reading In Tongues and Translating

Exodus 8:16 - Lice From The Dust of The Earth

And the LORD said unto Moses, Say unto Aaron, Stretch out thy rod, and smite the dust (Pokorny 261, dheu-(1), dhuno-, dhwene-, and dud- = Dove, the dark-colored bird/falcon, a representation of The Holy Ghost that Jehovah wants To disappear, To die so that he can deceive you with a false image) of the land, that it may become lice (H3654, ken = fixing or fastening your eyes on something until you gain an understanding of how to plant words like planting a vineyard and watch for what grows from the vine. The growth results in a CRIB or MANGER, which we know means the birth-bed of The Son of God) throughout all the land of Egypt (Egypt and Mizraim mean to be able to come together with God so that He may *"cause you to weigh or consider that which causes to oppress." In this case, you are watching to see what or who grows oppression/bondage/ slavery and as an Egyptian you are called to do something about it in order to relieve the anguish!)*

WORD STUDY

Dust = Dove = Falcon = Vineyard of Christ

Dust = Pokorny #261. dheu- = Dove, the dark colored bird

(Pokorny #261) dheu- = To rise in a cloud as dust, vapor, smoke, breath. Denotes various color adjectives and defective perception or wits. (1b) Spirit, soul. (6a) DUST (6b) Bird's down, "fine like dust.' (11a) Beclouded in the senses

(11b) DOVE, the dark-colored bird. (See: NIDIFY)

dhuno- = Pokorny #261, Fortified, enclosed place (See: SEIGE).

dhwene- = Pokorny #261, To disappear, die.

dud- = Pokorny #261, To shake, deceive.

The dark-colored bird is the Egyptian Falcon. See My YouTube video: WILL THE REAL HOLY GHOST PLEASE MANIFEST.

Lice = H18, 'ebuwc = A MANGER, crib

H3654. ken = from 3661 in the sense of fastening (fixing your eyes on something); a gnat (from infixing its sting; used only in plural (and irreg. in Exod. 8:17,18; Heb. 13:14)):--**lice**, X manner. See Hebrew 3661. See Hebrew 18.

H3661. kanan = a primitive root; to set out, i.e. plant:--X vineyard.

H18. 'ebuwc (ay-booce') = from 75; **A MANGER** or stall:--crib.

Christ, The Son of God/Pharaoh born in a manger.

Make Sure To Cross Reference With **SPIRITUAL BIPOLAR: GOD IS THE PEACE IN YOUR HEART THAT CALMS THE VOICES ABOVE YOUR HEAD.**

Page 52

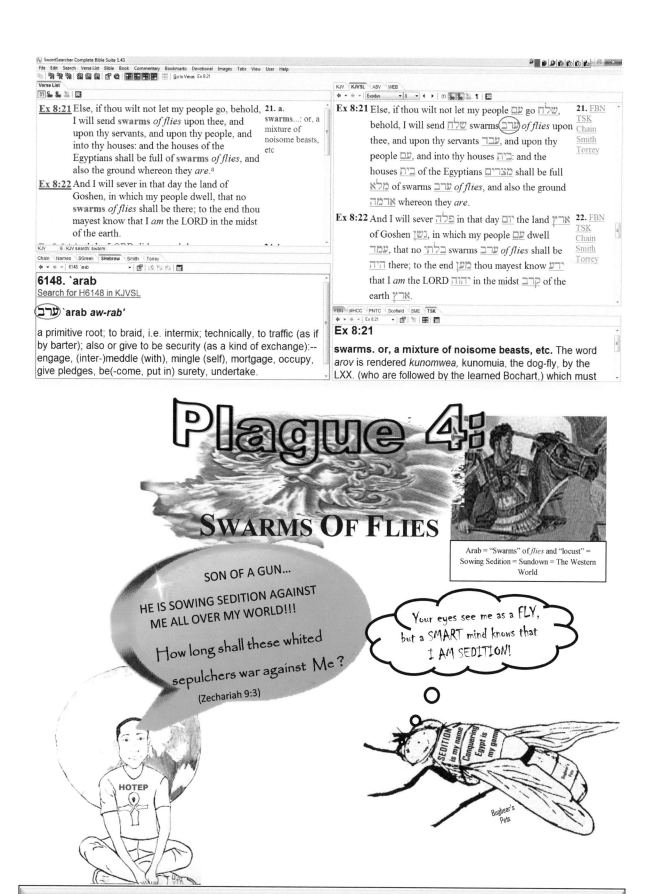

Visual Demonstration of Sedition

Before Jehovah the God of mischief can murder The Son of God and make it acceptable to the people of God, he must first turn the people of God against their ancestral Godhead so that they convert over to him. What is his plan of action for the usurpation and conversion?

✓ Sow Sedition

Come; let us *Read In Tongues* and have a closer look at the Scriptures with their definitions...

But first, I have anticipated your question: "What is Sedition?"

By explaining the plagues of "Lice From Dust of the Earth" and "Swarms" *of flies,* I will prove to you that Zeus/Jehovah/Satan's mission from the beginning has been to usurp yOur heavenly Kingdom, murder The Son of God/Pharaoh, and condemn His Hamitic Black peoples into bondage. Wordsmiths camouflaged these words so that their true interpretation may be revealed to you, the Redeemed, during this dispensation of My Second Coming.

Come Here, I will show you how SEDITION is done !

I, Jehovah, will teach the Atenites that The Aten is a heretic and a failure. He wipes away all other Gods and is the sole monotheistic God in human history. But I will steal his identity and attribute the practice of One God to myself. I will paint The Aten as God of a deformed madman. Then I will glorify myself and become the ONE GOD of all creation, effectively replacing The Aten. It is insurrection, rebellion, sedition, war in high places, but when I am done with The Aten, the Atenites will side with ME because I will MAKE them to lust after MY money that I and I alone control ! I will be God. The Aten will be despised and rejected! I, Jehovah the God of mischief, will be the LIGHT of the world. The Aten will be The Devil.

Don't Rise Up, Pharaoh, Son of God, Aten

Come to father God of mischief, little Black Atenite, Your people are evil, but I will adopt you and teach you to be good. And I will cause you to love MY people and MY money more than your own, okay. Come on...

aka Anti-Christ = Anti-Black

There is still more to learn...

Come Here, See, I will show you how Jehovah the God of mischief SOWS SEDITION through his money !

LOOK

Arab = "Swarms" and "locust" = Sowing Sedition = Sundown = The Western World

Luke 20:22- 25 and Luke 23:2

Is it lawful for us to give tribute unto Caesar, or no? But he *(Pharaoh)* perceived their craftiness, and said unto them, Why tempt ye me? Shew me a penny. Whose image and superscription hath it? They answered and said, Caesar's. And he said unto them, **Render** therefore unto Caesar the things which be Caesar's, and unto God the things which be God's…. And they began **To Accuse** him, saying, We *(accusers and oppressors)* found this *fellow (Pharaoh)* perverting the nation, and forbidding to give tribute to Caesar, saying that he himself is Christ a King.

The date of Christ/ *that fellow* Pharaoh is circa 6-4 BC. Somewhere during His adulthood, the Chief Priest and Scribe, *of Shem and Japheth* came to The Lord asking if it were lawful for them to "pay tribute," to Caesar (which means to "uphold" him)?

They say the Pharaoh forbade it.

Coins, bearing superscriptions of Zeus as God and Alexander and Caesar as his sons, were first minted between 359-269 BC. Remember, The Aten ruled in 1,300 BC. With the advent of Zeus' currency came the usurpation of the Hamitic Kingdom. What the Chiefs wanted from Christ/Pharaoh was for Him to submit and uphold Zeus by accepting Zeus' money and by bidding His Redeemed to do the same. Faithfully, He forbade it and The Pharaoh called for, and got, His money out of a fish's mouth. Otherwise, He would have committed SEDITION inside of His Own Kingdom and His house would have fallen. As it stands, because Christ got the VICTORY, today we can **transmute** Zeus'/Jehovah the God of mischief's money **over to The Aten** and not have SEDITIOUS offenses when Zeus' currency pass through our hands.

IT IS TIME TO STOP THEIR SEDITION AND TO STOP THEM FROM RENDERING MONEY TO THE DEVIL! LEARN HOW at http://angelapowell.wix.com/dethronejehovah

MONEY MYSTERY

"Alexander," "Locust," and "Spider" have the same etymon, which means that Alexander was one of the SOWERS OF SEDITON. He and Caesar minted coins with Zeus's images. The Western World's $1 dollar bill has a Greek spider on it to signify they uphold The Devil by **render**ing/ reinvesting Jehovah's Money right back to him {See: Page 80}.

Reading In Tongues and Translating

Exodus 8:19-24 Swarms

Then the magicians said unto Pharaoh (Son of God/Aten), This is the finger of God (Jehovah) *of mischief*: and Pharaoh's heart was hardened, and he hearkened not unto them; as the LORD had said. And the LORD said unto Moses (write an excerpt), Rise up early in the morning, and stand before Pharaoh; lo, he cometh forth to the water (hear intelligently); and say unto him, Thus saith the LORD, Let my people go, that they may serve me. Else, if thou wilt not let my people go, behold, I will send swarms of flies upon thee, and upon thy servants, and upon thy people, and into thy houses: and the houses of the Egyptians shall be full of swarms of flies, and also the ground whereon they are. And I will sever in that day the land of Goshen (approaching, drawing near), in which my people dwell, that no swarms of flies shall be there; to the end thou mayest know that I am the LORD in the midst of the earth. And I will put a division between my people and thy people: to morrow shall this sign be. And the LORD (Jehovah, God of mischief) did so; and there came a grievous swarm (H6148. ⁻arab = (Hitchcock Bible Names) Arab = sowing sedition; a locust; biblically, locust means a great army) *of flies* into the house of Pharaoh (Son of God), and into his servants' houses, and into all the land of Egypt (anguish, weigh oppression): the land (ashamed, disappointed) was corrupted by reason of the swarm (sedition) *of flies*. (NOTE: The emphasis is on "swarms" as *flies* is in italics and could mean anything from mosquitoes to any stinging or pesky insect like lice or flies.)

FACT 4

The God ATEN Who gave you the concept of "eternal life" foreknew you all would be born exactly AD 2000 – 2050. He knew you would have the Hieroglyphic books that would pictographically loose the wisdom needed to free you from bondage. Upon first glance, it may seem strange to see God depicted as a falcon. With understanding, you can now consider that "falcon" means "nidia," "nest," "dark-colored bird," which means "DOVE," which means "The Holy Ghost." Even though the depiction was give 10,000 – 5,000 years ago, this newly released knowledge about The Holy Ghost brings you right back home to the native roots and Godhead of your ancient ancestors.

WORD STUDY

Arab = Sowing Sedition

H6157. `arob = from 6148; a mosquito (from its swarming):--divers sorts of flies, swarm. See Hebrew 6148

H6148. `arab = a primitive root; to braid, i.e. intermix; technically, to traffic (as if by barter); also or give to be security (as a kind of exchange):--engage, (inter-)meddle (with), mingle (self), mortgage, occupy, give pledges, be(-come, put in) surety, undertake.

(Hitchcock Bible Names) Arab = multiplying; sowing sedition; a window; **a locust**, (biblically, locust means a great army).

Locust comes from Pokorny #32, and #673

Pokorny #32, alek- = To ward off, *or to* protect: ALEXANDER.

Pokorny #673, lek- = To leap, fly: LOCUST (spider), LOBSTER.

Sedition comes from Pokorny #882, s(w)e-
= where we again revisit the etymons for Mizraim.
Misraim is the biblical name for Egypt? **Mizraim** means **besiege places**.
Besiege comes from the word *"Siege,"* which means *"Throne,"* *"Falcon's Nest,"* and to be *"Created From One's Self,"* which means you are speaking about or learning about The Lord God Aten. And when you learn about YOUR Lord and His people, you must of necessity learn about Ancestors of the same kind as you.

Biblically, sedition is a reference to when one causes a division between an individual and his King and or his God(-s). It often means what the Chaldeans (okay, that's Abraham, Isaac, and Jacob//and locust = Alexander, which means the heirs of Shem and Japheth) did to Egypt and her people. Continually, they usurp our kingdom and enslave us.
IT IS TIME TO STOP THEM! LEARN HOW at
http://angelapowell.wix.com/dethronejehovah

TODAY'S REVELATION:

Using the etymons for "Dust," "Lice," and "Swarms," as written in Plagues 3 and 4, the only revelatory message to draw is that I, The Aten, Am showing you how Jehovah the God of mischief uses Abraham, Isaac, and Jacob, and Alexander the Great, who are the seed/image/ heirs of Shem and Japheth, to usurp/besiege the Throne of The Son of God and of The Holy Ghost.

Jehovah and his sorcerers and his Magicians sent out an army that has been "SOWING SEDITION" ever since Terah, Abraham's father, taught him to traffic Canaan/Egypt/Ham. They learned how to cast spells of sedition against The Son of God/Pharaoh, also they learned how to formulate an everlasting army capable of usurping both the African Continent and The Amen Covenant of Life. And they were, then, breed to be hateful enough to enforce the enslavement of African peoples.

The patriarchs of Shem and Japheth remained alive via reincarnation for up to a 1,000-years. They are Abraham's, and Isaac's, and Jacob's "gathered-souls" that guide them on how to strategically plague The Son of God and Egypt. Abraham was the first to "grievously plague Egypt." Moses's Ten Plagues are just a continuation of Jehovah the God of mischief and Abraham's plots to take over the Throne of The Aten and replace the real Holy Ghost, which is "the Dove, the dark-colored bird, which is The Egyptian Falcon" with a false idolatrous image of a white dove.

Make Sure To Cross Reference With **SPIRITUAL BIPOLAR: GOD IS THE PEACE IN YOUR HEART THAT CALMS THE VOICES ABOVE YOUR HEAD.**

Page 58

In order to bring about the death of
The Son of God, and to deceive you into
accepting the Godhead of Shem and Japheth,
dumbness, server grief, a stoppage of truth/maā-t, and a
furbish sword were sent throughout the African Continent.
The army that brandished the sword **sowed sedition** against your
Hamitic Godhead. They replaced the image of the real Holy
Ghost with an imposter, an idol. As a Christian, you are taught
that the only unforgivable sin that will sentence you to
everlasting damnation is to blasphemy The Holy Ghost.
Therefore, you do not want to question any aspect of The Holy
Ghost-- but you must. **Start by viewing My YouTube video:**
WILL THE REAL HOLY GHOST PLEASE MANIFEST.

After you watch WILL THE REAL HOLY GHOST PLEASE MANIFEST,
please watch ABRAHAM AND JEHOVAH'S THREE-FOLD CURSE OF
CAPTIVITY AGAINST THE BLACK MAN.

Both videos will help you more clearly understand this
Spirit-changing message from Me,
The Lord yOur God.

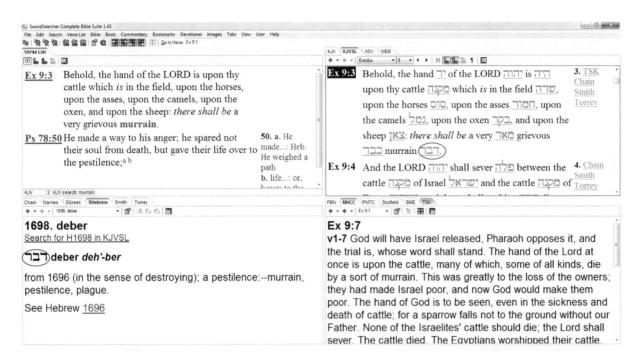

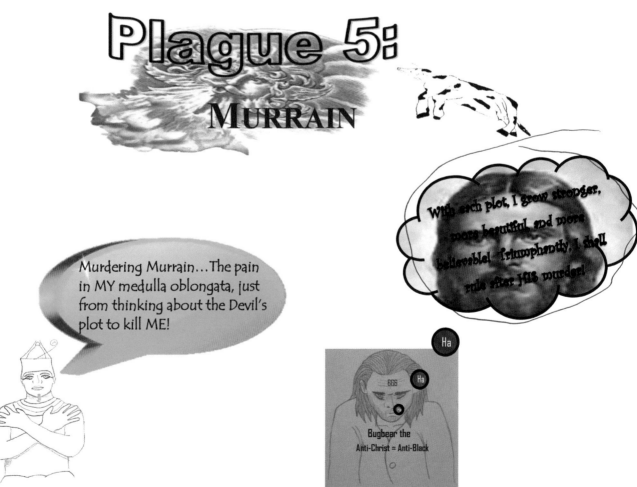

Plague 5: MURRAIN

Murdering Murrain...The pain in MY medulla oblongata, just from thinking about the Devil's plot to kill ME!

With each plot, I grow stronger, more beautiful and more believable! Triumphantly, I shall rule after HIS murder!

666
Ha
Ha

Bugbear the
Anti-Christ = Anti-Black

The Lord God Alpha Khen Omega Speaks

Jehovah the God of mischief sent forth an army carrying a furbished sword. They sowed sedition and installed a false image of The Holy Ghost to deceive the people of God. Anyone who can figure it out will overcome the state of dumbness that plagues the Hamitic people; but he may feel PAIN because:

- ✓ The anointing makes him **SMART**
- ✓ The anointing causes **PAIN** in the **medulla** oblongata of anyone SMART enough to look into the plagues placed on Egypt in order to get to the root of the death of Christ/Son of God/Pharaoh.

Come; let us *Read In Tongues* and have a closer look at the Scriptures with their definitions…

Exodus 9:3- 4 Grievous Murrai ∩

Behold, the hand of the LORD (Jehovah the God of mischief) is upon thy cattle (H4735. miqneh = something bought, property, livestock {chattel slavery}, from H7069. qanah, provoke to jealousy {See: Ezekiel 8:3}) which is in the field (H7704. sadeh = To spread out. (See: H774. 'Arpad = To Spread out) 'Arpad = The light of redemption [Hitchcock Bible Names]) upon the horses, upon the asses, upon the camels, upon the oxen, and upon the sheep: there shall be a very grievous murrain (Murder and subdue Christ/Son of God/Pharaoh, as well as those who are smart and anointed).

And the LORD shall sever between the cattle of Israel (he who wrestles with God) and the cattle of Egypt (He who weighs, consider that which causes Oppression and Anguish) and there shall nothing die of all that is the children's of Israel.

WORD STUDY

Plague = To Subdue, Murder = Christ = Son of God = Pharaoh and His People

Hebrew 1698. deber = from 1696 (in the sense of destroying); a pestilence:-- murrain, pestilence, plague. See Hebrew 1696

Hebrew 1696. dabar = a primitive root; perhaps properly, to arrange; but used figuratively (of words), to speak; rarely (in a destructive sense) **to subdue**:--etc.

Murrain: from *mori*, to die. See: Pokorny, mer-[(2)]

Pokorny #735, mer-[(2)] = To rub away, harm. To die. Murder. Nightmare, goblin, incubus, etc. See: smerd-.

Pokorny #970, smerd- = Pain. To be painful, SMART.

Pokorny #970, smer-[(3)] = Grease, fat: 1a. **SMEAR**. 1b. Apply salve. 3. MEDULLA.

SMEAR = [Middle English *smeren*, to anoint, from Old English *smerian*.] See: **ghrêi-**

Pokorny 457, **ghrêi-**. Important derivatives are: *grisly, grime, Christ, christen, Christian,* and *Christmas*.
To rub. **1.** GRISLY, from Old English *grislîc*, terrifying, from Germanic *gris-*, to frighten (< "to grate on the mind"). **2.** GRIME, from Middle English *grime*, grime, from a source akin to Middle Dutch *grime*, grime, from Germanic *grìm-*, **smear**. **3.** Extended form *ghrìs-*. CHRISM, CHRIST, (CHRISTEN), (CHRISTIAN); (CHRISTMAS), CREAM, from Greek *khriein*, to anoint. [Pokorny *ghrêi-* 457.]

TODAY'S REVELATION:

Murrain! = Are you SMART
enough to know why "CHRIST" died?
Can you handle the truth? The answer is right
here in Plague 5, the curse of the "grievous murrain."
It is a word that "grates the mind" until it creates that
anointing to make you understand Plague 5 foreshadows
the death of Christ. Christ is The Son of God. Son of God means
Pharaoh. Pharaoh is the man-Son of God in the earth, but even
though He is in the shape of a man, He is how we teach of Christ that
He is both Son of God and God. He is both human and divine; both God
and man at the same time. He believes in Eternal Life much in the same
manner as Christ said, "If you believe in Me, you shall never die" because His
Spirit is forever alive. He brings you into Eternal Life, which is His "REST."

You are in the age where this Son of God is showing you how to look back
in time to reinterpret the 10 Plagues so that you may know what to expect
in the future and know what to do about it. You need to know that the
plagues curse you into bondage. I Am here to show you how to come out
of the bondage by turning away from Jehovah, Abraham, Isaac, and Jacob
and their Covenant of Death and Hell. Your covenant is The Amen
Covenant of Life. You have to pray to Me, The Lord God Alpha Khen
Omega to reinstate Life and overcome and annihilate the Death, as is written
in Revelation 20:14.

With Plague 1, Jehovah the God of mischief makes you dumb. In
Plague 5, he foreshadows the death of Christ and taunts you to be
SMART enough to figure out how he plans to murder
The Son of God/Pharaoh. We know The Christ was
crucified; the question is: How are you going to help
your God make The Devil and his heirs
honor the work of The Cross, which
is "to set free the enslaved?"

Make Sure To Cross Reference With **SPIRITUAL BIPOLAR: GOD IS THE PEACE IN YOUR HEART THAT CALMS THE VOICES ABOVE YOUR HEAD.**

Page 64

THE POWER OF *Writing*

Down My Thoughts

1. Study Plagues 1-10. From the list of definitions, write down a few words that will **explain the stages** of each curse Jehovah the God of mischief placed on Egypt. Compare you answers to The Aten Converter's answers that are found on page 96.

1.

2.

3.

4.

5.

6.

7.

8.

9.

10.

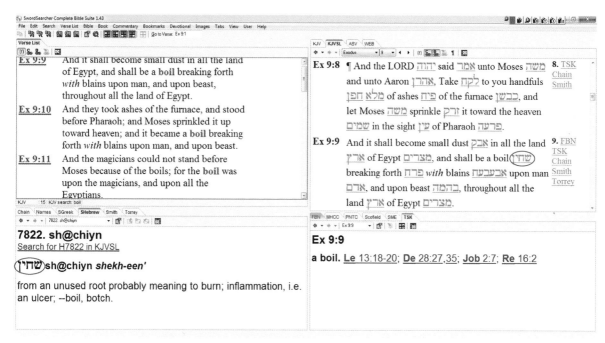

Plague 6:
BOILS WITH BLAINS

BOILS...and BLAINS... with BONDAGE!! ...WHAT DAH...?

Hear me well, oh seed of Ham, just as surely as those boils shall burst, I shall bring upon you 400 years of bondage...not once... not twice...but trice!

All ten plagues are physical, but in order for you to understand them, you have to comprehend what transpired spiritually when Jacob **"wrestled with God."** Wordsmiths use the word "bedust" to describe the match. It means:

- ✓ To be able to speak words that will ensnare one
- ✓ Have power to bring the people of God into bondage

Come; let us *Read In Tongues* and have a closer look at the Scriptures with their definitions...

Exodus 9:8- 9   Boils With Blains

And the LORD said unto Moses and unto Aaron, Take to you handfuls of ashes (H6368. piyach, from 6315; a powder (as easily puffed away), i.e. ashes or dust:--ashes. See Hebrew 6315. Puwach = a primitive root; to puff, i.e. blow with the breath or air; plague; speak, utter words to bring into a snare,) of the furnace (3536. kibshan = from 3533; a smelting furnace (as reducing metals):-- Hebrew 3533. Kabash = a primitive root; to tread down; bring into bondage, keep under, bring into subjection), and let Moses sprinkle it toward the heaven in the sight of Pharaoh. And it shall become small dust (79. 'abaq = a primitive root, probably to float away (as vapor), but used only as denominative from 80; to bedust, i.e. grapple:-- wrestle. See Hebrew 80, 'abaq = from root of 79; light particles (as volatile):--(small) dust, powder.) in all the land of Egypt, and shall be a boil breaking forth with blains (H1564. GOLEM = Embryo - See: Psalms 139 and 2Kings 2:8) upon man, and upon beast, throughout all the land of Egypt.

WORD STUDY

Bedust = To Wrestle With God or Light Particles

79. 'abaq = a primitive root, probably to float away (as vapor), but used only as denominative from 80; to bedust, i.e. grapple:-- wrestle// See Hebrew 80

80. 'abaq = from root of 79; light particles (as volatile):--(small) dust, powder// See Hebrew 79

watt/mark

I, The Aten, shall give you power to fight against Jehovah, Abraham, Isaac, and Jacob. You shall bedust them and win, which means wrestle against them in spiritual warfare that takes place first in your mind, the MEDULLA.

Paul of Tarsus

Joseph

Jacob

Isaac

Zeus/Jehovah/Adversary

Abraham

TODAY'S REVELATION:

Moses has to sprinkle ash towards heaven in the sight of The Son of God and this ash becomes small dust. In other verses the word "dust" means the "dove, the dark-colored bird;" but in this verse, "dust" means to "bedust," and it comes from H79 and H80, abaq. It is only used in Genesis 32:25-28 to describe the wrestling match between Jacob/Israel and God

Jacob got his power and strength to fight against the Creator God from Jehovah the God of mischief. During the Second Coming, when you are ready to convert, I, The Aten, shall give you power to fight against Jehovah, Abraham, Isaac, and Jacob. You shall "bedust" them, which means wrestle against them in spiritual warfare that takes place first in your mind, the MEDULLA.

The God of mischief goes on to tell Moses and Aaron that the ashes and dust shall become a boil with blains. The word that the wordsmith uses is H1564, g olem. Golem is one of those unique words like "bedust," in that it is only used once. Golem is used in Psalms 139 when the King speaks to God about being wonderfully and fearfully made. The scholars say this Psalms is about an embryo. Golem is also used in 2Kings 2:8 when Elijah uses his mantle to part the waters of Jordan. Jehovah the God of mischief utters words to ensnare you in captivity before you spring forth of your mother's wombs. But I, The Aten, The Lord your God grow you up in the mantle of Elijah, so that you may break the yokes of bondage that Noah placed on you.

SPIRITUAL BIPOLAR Make Sure To Cross Reference With **SPIRITUAL BIPOLAR: GOD IS THE PEACE IN YOUR HEART THAT CALMS THE VOICES ABOVE YOUR HEAD.**

Page 70

I, The Aten, Am showing you that by
taking ash from the furnace, the Wicked Ones
cast spells, either by action or utterance, that are meant
to bring you into bondage and keep you under subjection
from the time you are conceived in your mother's womb up
until the time you become like Elijah, having power with God to
perform supernatural acts that will break Shem's and Japheth's
spells and conjurations.   The operative word used in this battle
between you and evil spirits is "bedust." Bedust is only used to describe the
mystical wrestling match between Jacob/Israel and God. Scholars describe the
battle as a test of wills between spirits that are "light particles" or "flying spirits"
visible only in your mind. Pokorny etymologists assign the words
"Poltergeists," "Incubus," "Goblins," and "Nightmare" when identifying these
evils spirits and defining the struggles they put you through in order to gain
control over your mind and rule over you as God. Jacob/Israel *is now* a "light
particle." His name means "He who wrestles with God, and he will rule as God."
Jacob/Israel/Jehovah comes to wrestle with you when you attempt to convert
to Me, The Aten, the True God and Creator. If Israel/Jehovah subdue your
mind, the wrestling match is over and they continue to have the rule over you
even before you realize that they are the "Wicked Ones" who hold the seed of
Ham in bondage. This is so deep! It is just the beginning exegesis of
Redemption for the sons of Ham. Jehovah the God of mischief use the
Ten Plagues as evil; but today, I, The Aten, Am showing you how to
reinterpret the plagues to see the spells that Jehovah cast upon us
and how to reverse the hands of His evil deeds so that the
masters of captivity may be bound in captivity
themselves under the mighty hand of
The Lord God Alpha Khen Omega
(Revelation 13:10).

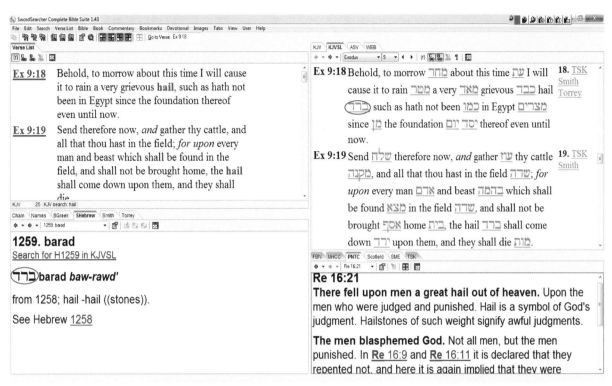

First, Jehovah the God of mischief forecasts his intent to ensnare and bring the people of God into bondage. Then, he strikes with punitory hail. The significance of hail is to:

- ✓ Actually seize and snatch the Black Egyptians
- ✓ Rob them until they are bankrupt and naked
- ✓ Prepare them for a "Rapture," which will ensure a future time of captivity

Come; let us *Read In Tongues* and have a closer look at the Scriptures with their definitions…

Exodus 9:18-19   Hail Mingled With Fire

Behold, to morrow about this time I will cause it to rain a very grievous hail (Pokorny #518, kaghlo- = Hail. Pokorny #518, kagh- = To Capture, Seize, falconry), such as hath not been in Egypt (weighting what causes oppression) since the foundation (H3117. yowm = To be hot; from H2552. chamam = To be hot; from H2525. cham = hot; from H2526. Cham = Ham, his descendants or their country) + (H3245. yacad = To take counsel, instruct, ordain; meaning: To sit down together as Ham) thereof even until now.

Send therefore now, and gather thy cattle (chattel slavery; seat of jealousy), and all that thou hast in the field (Redemption); for upon every man and beast which shall be found in the field (Redemption), and shall not be brought home, the hail (Capture, Seize, Falconry) shall come down upon them, and they shall die (Lose Pharaonic/ Son of God/Christ-ian anointing).

WORD STUDY

Hail = Seize = To snatch = Usurp

Pokorny #518, kaghlo- = Pebble. Hail.

Pokorny #518, kagh- = To Catch, **Seize**; wickerwork, fence. 1. Germanic *hag-* in: a. Old French haggard, wild hawk (< "raptor"): HAGGARD- a wild adult hawk captured for training; falconry. {You are being trained "To Seize" Jehovah the God of mischief}.

"<u>TO SEIZE</u>" = **rep-**. Important derivatives are: *rape[1], rapid, rapt, ravish,* and *SURREPTITIOUS*.

To snatch. Suffixed zero-grade form *rap-yo-*. RAPACIOUS, RAPE[1], RAPID, RAPINE, RAPT (RAPTURE), (RAVEN[2]), RAVIN, RAVISH; EREPSIN, (SUBREPTION), *SURREPTITIOUS*, from Latin *rapere*, <u>to seize</u>. [Pokorny *rep-* 865.]

#865, rep-(1) = To Creep {*as in serpent/Devil*}, Slink: REPTILE

#865, rendh- = To tear up: REND (< "thing torn off") RIND

<u>TO SNATCH</u>" = **reup-**. Important derivatives are: *robe, usurp, bankrupt, etc.*

Also **reub-** . To snatch.
II. O-grade form *roup-*. **1. c.** ROVER[2], from Middle Dutch and Middle Low German *roven*, to rob. **3.** ROBE, from Old French *robe*, robe (< "clothes taken as booty" {*as in Christ's stolen robe}*), from Germanic *raubo*, booty.
III. Zero-grade form *rup-*. **1.** USURP, from Latin *úsúrpâre* (< *úsu-rup-*; *úsus*, use, usage, from *úti*, to use), originally "to interrupt the orderly acquisition of something by the act of using," whence to take into use, usurp. **2.** Nasalized BANKRUPT, from Latin *rumpere*, to break. [Pokorny 2. *reu-* 868.]

#868, ruk-[(2)] = Rough, To Scrape, To Dig: ORC/ORCA {as in Jonah and whale}

ROVER[2] = Spirit, Opportunity, and Curiosity Rovers Martian

TODAY'S REVELATION:

The Lord God Alpha Khen Omega Speaks

In Exodus, chapter 9:14-16, for the 7th Plague, Jehovah the God of mischief plans "to smite The Son of God and the Black Egyptians with so much hardship, with so much shame and confusion of face, and with so much entrapment that causes sin and bondage that we shall live like dead men until we are "cut off from the entire Earth." Jehovah said, "For this cause have I raised thee up," which means he is telling us that he hardened the heart of The Son of God/Pharaoh to go into battle against him so that he could make a name for himself and become God to the Egyptian people instead of Me, The Aten. From the time Jehovah turns water into blood up till the death of the first born son, he successfully implements agendas favorable to usurping the throne of The Son of God, which means Sa Ra and Pharaoh.

Early on in this book, I showed you Scriptures which state the Hebrews held the Egyptians in bondage and that those Hebrews were first called Assyrians. They hail from Ur of the Chaldees, which means the place of the occults and dark forces. They are sorcerers and they are the heirs of Jehovah and Shem and Japheth. In order for them to prosper and gain a name, a kingdom, and dominion for their Gods of mischief and themselves, they must fulfill Noah's curse of captivity against Canaan/Ham/Egypt, which does in fact "cut off the Black Pharaoh and Black Egyptians from existence." But in spite of what Jehovah is doing to you, for this present moment, I want you to refocus your attention on a message from Me, The Aten. To clearly see the camouflage lesson behind "hail mingled with fire," you must reinterpret the Hebrew tongue using your English tongue. The Serpent, also called the Dragon and Satan the Devil, which is Zeus and Jehovah the God of mischief, causes insurrection against Me, The Aten, and usurps My Kingdom, for which cause he is bound in the prison of a bottomless pit for a 1,000 years. After which, he shall be loosed for a little season to deceive the nations which are in the four quarters of the earth, Gog and Magog, to gather them together to battle against Me, The Lord God AlphaKhenOmega.

By faith, I rend Jehovah's rovers.

The people against Me number as the sand of the sea for multitude. (Coincidentally, that is also the number of the seed of Abraham). When this multitude **seizes** upon the Egyptians, "they spoil the Egyptians." **Spoil** has an etymon meaning "snatch away." Think about what that choice-word from the wordsmith tells you. They kidnap the Egyptians or, via trickery, force the Redeemed into following them out of the land of Ham. They plunder the Redeemed's silver and gold and all their precious jewelry and fine linen apparel. They put on these unique Egyptian identifiers and when they (Abraham's multitude) leave out of Egypt, they are no more Shemetic or Japhetic; they become **corrupt and degenerate White Egyptians**. Therefore, when it becomes time for salvation, these same Shemetic and Japhetic Chirst-ian heirs **snatch the robe** of The Son of God/Pharaoh and hold it as **booty** to signify their Kingdom **usurpation** is complete. And for all practical purposes, the transformation and the usurpation are finished. The seed of Ham, the true Black Egyptian is homeless. He does not know why he is without a sovereign homeland, nor does he know why he is in captivity. I will go so far as to say the only God that those of Ham know is Jehovah the God of mischief, and they believe he is the Great God and Father of all, that he has no respect of persons, and that he is their Redeemer. If you are one who believes all of the above, I, The Lord God Alpha Khen Omega, must pose a question to you: **"Why were your people kidnapped (Raptured) and enslaved? What is to stop it from happening again?"** And it shall happen again, this time on the Planet Mars. If Shem and Japheth make it up there before Africans collectively convert over to The Lord God Alpha Khen Omega, we shall again become their slaves. Their rovers named Spirit, Opportunity, and Curiosity are already paving the way for Martian habitation. Their prophesy is that by the years 2020-2050, Shem and Japheth shall colonize and live on the barren planet. That gives you, the Redeemed seed of Ham, all of five-to-thirty-years to **BANKRUPT** Jehovah. You must allow Me, The Aten-in-My-new name- The Lord God Alpha Khen Omega, to train you like a falcon to go out and **seize Jehovah** until you **REND** his **rovers**,

Isaiah 28:14-19

tear up his Abrahamic Covenant of Death and Hell (Isaiah 28:14-17), and **usurp** his kingdom, *just like he did to* yOurs, until he is utterly **broken** and **BANKRUPT**.

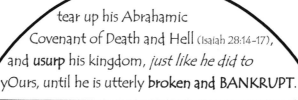

To learn how, See My video: Money To The Bank Parable (Luke 19:23): Take Back Your Wealth, also Stop by:
http://angelapowell.wix.com/dethronejehovah

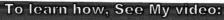

Now that the plagues ensnare the Black Hamitic seed into bondage via the **Rapture**, what do you suppose Jehovah the God of mischief will conjure up in the next plague of locust to ensure the fulfillment of his maledictions?

By faith, I bankrupt, Zeus/Jehovah.

FACT 5

The contentious debate over: "Are the ancient/aboriginal Egyptians Black or White?" stems from White men like Abraham, Saul-Paul of Tarsus, Alexander, and the Euro-image of Jesus declaring themselves to be Hamitic/Egyptian/African/Black, *much like how Rachel Dolezal and other Whites put on Black-face and declare themselves as Black to ultimately obtain entry into God's REST by force and deception.* By-and-by, in the long run, after usurpation, foreign Egyptians have become the NEW BLACK, which is White! As a result, most Black children identify/love "the enemy" more than the true FATHER!

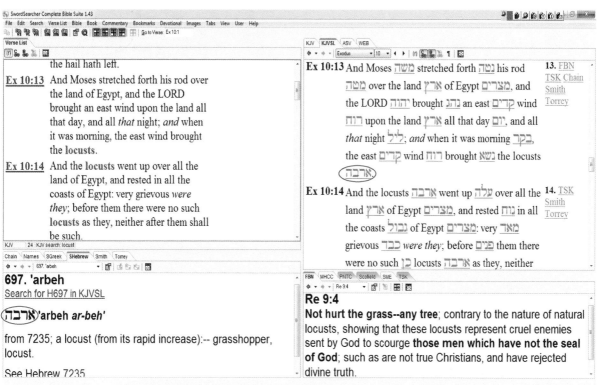

Plague 8:

LOCUST FROM THE EAST WIND

MOURNING DOVE... IT IS THE DESTROYER

They believe I am harmless... not a DESTROYER. And when you tell them, they won't believe YOU, Thou, Pharaoh, Son of God, because I have already painted You as the evil villain...LOL..Ha-Ha-Ha!

Egyptian Eye

Locusts = The Destroyer

Destroyer is the name of

✓ Alexander the Great
✓ Abaddon
✓ Apollyon ⟩ Revelation 9:11
✓ The Dove = Jonah

Come; let us *Read In Tongues* and have a closer look at the Scriptures with their definitions...

https://en.wikipedia.org/wiki/File:Mount_Kilimanjaro_2007.jpg// Mount Kilimanjaro from the air. July 2007. Photo by Lee R. Berger

250 mph

verily verily *INTERESTING*

Peregrine Falcons are the fastest animals on earth. They soar 15,000 thousands + feet up into the firmament; then they **dive** to catch their prey. That's almost three miles up in the air. It is like descending from the highest peak of Mount Kilimanjaro at a speed of 250 mph in mere seconds!

Dove Parable	
Verb Usage:	
Present Tense	Past Tense
Dive	**Dove**

30 Seconds To Capture

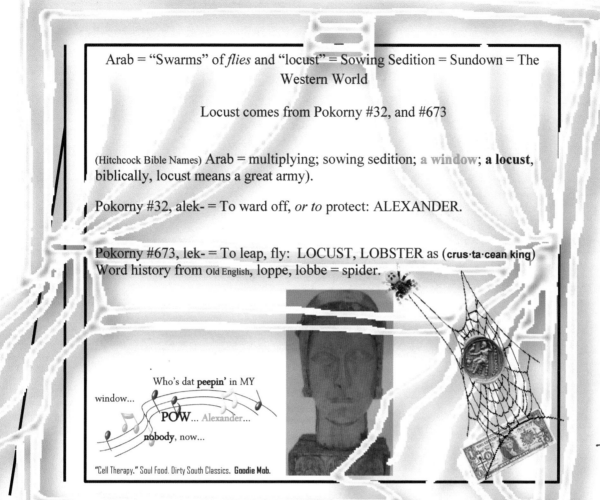

Arab = "Swarms" of *flies* and "locust" = Sowing Sedition = Sundown = The Western World

Locust comes from Pokorny #32, and #673

(Hitchcock Bible Names) Arab = multiplying; sowing sedition; a window; a locust, biblically, locust means a great army).

Pokorny #32, alek- = To ward off, *or to* protect: ALEXANDER.

Pokorny #673, lek- = To leap, fly: LOCUST, LOBSTER as (crus·ta·cean king) Word history from Old English, loppe, lobbe = spider.

Who's dat **peepin'** in MY window... **POW**... Alexander... **nobody**, now...

"Cell Therapy." Soul Food. Dirty South Classics. **Goodie Mob.**

FACT 6

Alexander the great is known for his entrance into Egypt (around 332 BC) whereby he met "no resistance" from neither the Egyptian nor the Persians nor the Macedonian peoples, which allowed him "to conquer all." (Abraham, then the Persians had already strong-armed Egypt from 552 to 332 BC. Afterwards from 332 BC to present AD 2015, Greeks, Romans, Macedonian, Persian, Arabian, Islamic, Turkish, Ottoman, French and WESTERN WORLD peoples SNATCHED UP Egypt). Alexander declared himself "Son of Zeus" and became "Savior of Egypt." He then divided Egypt between Egyptian and Grecian control. Architects built a city for him and called it Alexandria, which was the start of a White-washed Egypt.

Today, Are you one who will "protect" Alexander's spiritual rights to Conquer Egypt/Ham or will you "ward off"/bind his spirit?

TODAY'S REVELATION:

You may recall from Plague 4, the word "locust" comes from a Hebrew etymon "arab," meaning "sowing sedition." It is a reference to a great Chaldean army. Abraham is Chaldean. Shem and Japheth, though they are Hebrew/Jew and Greek or Caucasoid, are ethnic-Chaldeans. They now hail from the Western World. They sow sedition against Hamitic Divinity so that those of the seed of Ham turn away from their own Godhead, in order to worship Abraham's God of mischief, who is Jehovah. Their seditious archway reaches into this generation, causing you to resist and rebel against The Kingdom of The Aten. I Am not a mythological being as taught by Shem and Japheth. I Am alive, and My new name is The Lord God Alpha Khen Omega. Call on ME.

Religion says "No Other Gods Before Me," and makes it damnable to even utter the names of other Gods, which creates torment and fear.

Spirituality says "Let me compare the works of all other Gods so that I may find the true God of perfect love. Perfect Love casts out fear because fear causes torment (1John 4:18)."

Make Sure To Cross Reference With **SPIRITUAL BIPOLAR: GOD IS THE PEACE IN YOUR HEART THAT CALMS THE VOICES ABOVE YOUR HEAD.**

Page 82

The English etymons for
"Locusts" are Pokorny #32, and #673.
Pokorny #32, alek- = *To* protect or
To ward off **ALEXANDER**. But instead of discussing
Alexander, let us focus on the **locust** from the bottomless
pit (Revelation 9:1-12). These locusts have a king over them whose
name in Hebrew is Abaddon and in Greek is Apollyon. In both
tongues, the name means **"Destroyer."** Hmmm, verily verily
interesting! This calls for a special book and video all of its own!
You must SEE My video: WILL THE REAL HOLY GHOST PLEASE MANIFEST.
The name "Destroyer" comes from the name "Jonah," which also means
"Dove." In the Western World an image of a white dove represents The
Holy Ghost. It is an idol and a graven image (Deuteronomy De 7:5)!

From your study of Plague 3, "lice from the dust of the land," you learned
that the etymons for **"Dove"** describe it as **a dark-colored bird, which is the
Egyptian falcon that the Shemetic and Japhetic etymologists want "To
make disappear," "To die" because it has the power To shake ones faith, and
power To reveal one's deceptive religion.** This is a delicate subject, so let Me
again refer you to My video: WILL THE REAL HOLY GHOST PLEASE MANIFEST.
This video will surely take away the deception that keeps you bound for
thousands of years, though you and your people fancy themselves freemen.

Whereas the locusts in the Exodus plagues were commanded to destroy
all the herbs and plants of the field, and all the fruit trees, the locusts of
Revelation are commanded not to harm any green thing but to
only torment those men who do not have the seal of God in their
forehead (Revelation 9:4). What is the seal of God that is going to
protect you from the Destroyer? Remember Destroyer means
locusts, which means a great army sowing sedition against
Me, The Aten, and the real Holy Ghost, which is the
Egyptian Falcon. This great mystery revealing the seal
is only for the Elect,
the 144,000 Redeemed seed of Ham.
The Seal is:

Seal of God

Great Light

Àakhu = The Great Light; i.e., the sun
(Egyptian Hieroglyphic Dictionary, Vol. I, page 23a.)

Àakhu-en-Aten (Amen-hetep IV),
(Egyptian Hieroglyphic Dictionary, Vol. II, page 1257a.)

My historical name is: Re-Harakhti-in-his-name-Shu-who is Aten.

Today, I Am: The Aten-in-My-new name- The Lord God Alpha Khen Omega.

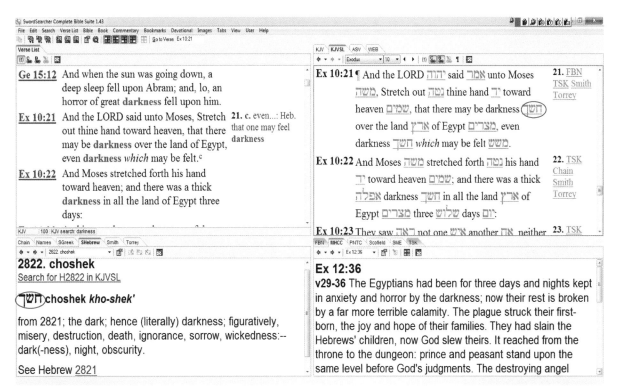

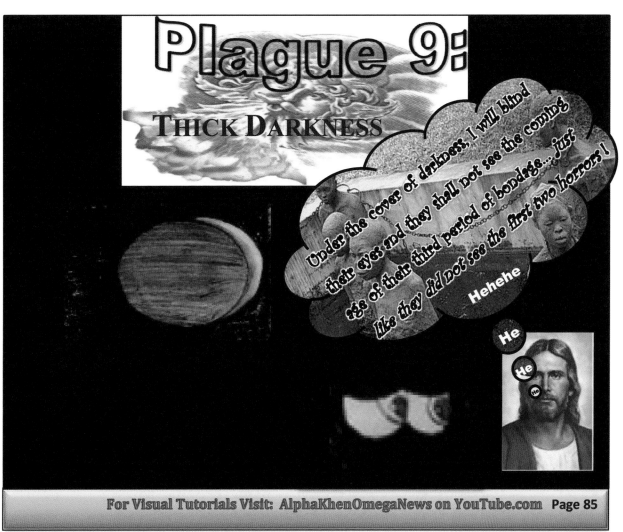

Four Words: Horror = Idol = Bugbear = Jehovah

✓ Jehovah the God of mischief makes it known that he causes four-hundred years of slavery.

✓ The Hebrew who just happen to be Chaldeans who just happen to be the heirs of Shem and Japheth are the ones who enslaved the Black Egyptian/Hamitic seed on behalf of Jehovah.

✓ The Egyptians were in darkness for three days, which means….Captivity X 3

Come; let us *Read In Tongues* and have a closer look at the Scriptures with their definitions…

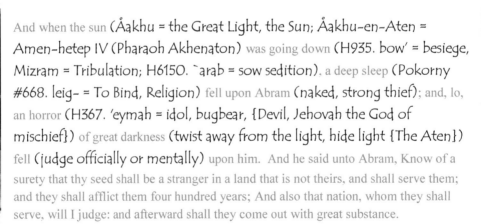

Genesis 15:12 - 14 and Exodus 10:21- 23
Horror of Great Darkness

And when the sun (Åakhu = the Great Light, the Sun; Åakhu-en-Aten = Amen-hetep IV (Pharaoh Akhenaton) was going down (H935. bow' = besiege, Mizram = Tribulation; H6150. ʿarab = sow sedition), a deep sleep (Pokorny #668. leig- = To Bind, Religion) fell upon Abram (naked, strong thief); and, lo, an horror (H367. ʿeymah = idol, bugbear, {Devil, Jehovah the God of mischief}) of great darkness (twist away from the light, hide light {The Aten}) fell (judge officially or mentally) upon him. And he said unto Abram, Know of a surety that thy seed shall be a stranger in a land that is not theirs, and shall serve them; and they shall afflict them four hundred years; And also that nation, whom they shall serve, will I judge: and afterward shall they come out with great substance.

And the LORD said unto Moses (draw, write an excerpt), Stretch out thine hand toward heaven (hear intelligently), that there may be darkness (twist away from the light, hide light {The Aten}) over the land of Egypt (weigh that which causes anguish and oppression), even darkness which may be felt. And Moses stretched forth his hand toward heaven; and there was a thick darkness in all the land of Egypt three (thrice) days (Aramaic . yowm = times): They saw not one another, neither rose any from his place for three days: but all the children of Israel had light in their dwellings.

Make Sure To Cross Reference With **SPIRITUAL BIPOLAR: GOD IS THE PEACE IN YOUR HEART THAT CALMS THE VOICES ABOVE YOUR HEAD.**

Page 86

Captive's Log

In regards to Abraham and his Covenant of Death and Hell, the word "darkness" is used to describe the scene where the sun, The Aten, is going down;

The etymon for the word **"HORROR"** is **"IDOL,"** and **"BUGBEAR,"** which means **"DEVIL."** Next, Jehovah the God of mischief, being referenced as that devil, appears to tell Abraham that he shall be afflicted with servitude for 400 years. Ergo, we find the cause of the Exodus story. Supposedly, the Hebrews have been enslaved in Egypt by Egyptians for 400 years. They cry out to their God and he comes to deliver them. Howbeit, there is a twist to the story. It takes a falcon's eye to spot it.

The Book of Isaiah says the Assyrians held the people of God in captivity (Isiah 52:4). The Assyrians are the Chaldeans, meaning Abraham, Isaac, and Jacob. The Bible says there are only seventy-two souls accounted to Jacob in the land of Egypt. They multiply to 600,000 footmen upon exiting Egypt. The rest of the people (who are enslaved) are a great mixed multitude from various tribes of Ham. They sold their land, their resources, and then their bodies into bondage so that they could live and not die during a famine that Jehovah causes.

Reread the story and pay close attention to the details. You will now be able to see the biblical account of slavery is vice versa to how the heirs of Shem and Japheth teach that they were slaves in Egypt. The real truth is the Hebrews enslave the Hamitic seed… Now that the story is switched back to its truth, Redemption from The Aten is at hand.

Captive's Log

The Hebrews, let's call them who they are…Shem and Japheth…have enslaved the seed of Ham…not once…but twice…and if they make it to Mars…they shall do it a third time. REFER TO MY VIDEO: JEHOVAH AND ABRAHAM'S THREE-FOLD CURSE OF CAPTIVITY AGAINST THE BLACK MAN.

God's questions to you are, "If you, ~~being the descendent~~ of the nativity of Ham, are from those forced into bondage, what are you going to do to free yourself?"

"How" and "where" are you going to seek Redemption when the enemy tries to enslave you on Mars?"

PLEASE, WRITE YOUR ANSWER.

_____

_____

_____

_____

_____

_____

_____

_____

Shem and Japheth have the Redeemed so deceived that they make us think "Redemption" applies to all men who are "slaves to sin."

---DO NOT BE DECEIVED---

Redemption means you need redeeming because you have a physical yoke of bondage around your neck, chocking you to death, because Shem, Japheth, and Jehovah their God of mischief put it there to make you a servant of servants, even into perpetuity.

So where will you turn for Redemption? Jesus Christ, the Son of God?

Captive's Log

That name "Jesus" just means "Deliverer," "To get victory," and "To be {set} free." His story is about a Deliverer, Who is a Son of God. He is a "Sa Ra," a "Son of Re," a Pharaoh! He says, "Seek My face (2Chronicles 7:14; Psalms 27:8)."

So, Whose "face" do you see? And, which "Son of God" will you turn too and serve (Revelation 22:3-4)?

PLEASE, WRITE YOUR ANSWER.

_____

_____

_____

_____

_____

_____

_____

I see the face of Pharaoh Akhenaton, Who is The Aten-in-His-New Name- The Lord God Alpha Khen Omega. He appears to me in His flesh, as He is, to teach me about the truth that destroys the yoke of bondage. Therefore, I serve Him; and He orders my steps with a Cross of Life, the ankh. The ankh gives me the ability to choose good over evil, Life over Death.

Now it is your turn!

PUT WHAT YOU ARE READING TO PRAYER!

Then become a doer of the word… **RESEARCH** what you are learning; and pray about it until you sweat great drops of sweat like blood!

WORD STUDY

Horror = Idol = Bugbear = Jehovah

Hebrew 367. 'eymah

or (shortened) remah {ay-maw'}; from the same as 366; fright; concrete, an idol **(as a bugbear)**:--dread, fear, horror, idol, terrible, terror. See Hebrew 366

bug·bear
1. A bugaboo.
2. A fearsome imaginary creature, especially one evoked to frighten children.
3. *bwg(a),* Ghost, The Devil

[Obsolete *bug*, hobgoblin (from Middle English *bugge*) + bear2.]

Make Sure To Cross Reference With **SPIRITUAL BIPOLAR: GOD IS THE PEACE IN YOUR HEART THAT CALMS THE VOICES ABOVE YOUR HEAD.**

Page 90

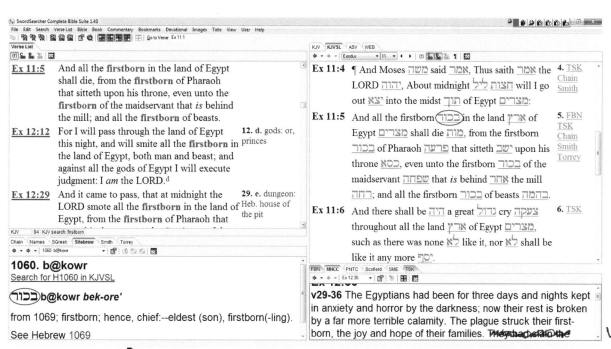

SwordSearcher Complete Bible Suite 1.43

File Edit Search Verse List Bible Book Commentary Bookmarks Devotional Images Tabs View User Help

Go to Verse: Ex 11:1

Verse List

Ex 11:5 And all the **firstborn** in the land of Egypt shall die, from the **firstborn** of Pharaoh that sitteth upon his throne, even unto the **firstborn** of the maidservant that *is* behind the mill; and all the **firstborn** of beasts.

Ex 12:12 For I will pass through the land of Egypt this night, and will smite all the **firstborn** in the land of Egypt, both man and beast; and against all the gods of Egypt I will execute judgment: I *am* the LORD.[d]   12. d. gods: or, princes

Ex 12:29 And it came to pass, that at midnight the LORD smote all the **firstborn** in the land of Egypt, from the **firstborn** of Pharaoh that   29. e. dungeon: Heb. house of the pit

KJV   94 KJV search: firstborn

Chain | Names | SGreek | SHebrew | Smith | Torrey
1060. b@kowr

1060. b@kowr

Search for H1060 in KJVSL

בכור **b@kowr** *bek-ore'*

from 1069; firstborn; hence, chief:--eldest (son), firstborn(-ling).

See Hebrew 1069

KJV | KJVSL | ASV | WEB

Exodus | 11

Ex 11:4 ¶ And Moses משה said אמר, Thus saith אמר the LORD יהוה, About midnight חצות ליל will I go out יצא into the midst תוך of Egypt מצרים: 4. TSK Chain Smith

Ex 11:5 And all the firstborn בכור in the land ארץ of Egypt מצרים shall die מות, from the firstborn בכור of Pharaoh פרעה that sitteth ישב upon his throne כסא, even unto the firstborn בכור of the maidservant שפחה that *is* behind אחר the mill רחה; and all the firstborn בכור of beasts בהמה.   5. FBN TSK Chain Smith Torrey

Ex 11:6 And there shall be היה a great גדול cry צעקה throughout all the land ארץ of Egypt מצרים, such as there was none לא like it, nor לא shall be like it any more יסף.   6. TSK

FBN | MHCC | PNTC | Scofield | SME | TSK

Ex 12:35

v29-36 The Egyptians had been for three days and nights kept in anxiety and horror by the darkness; now their rest is broken by a far more terrible calamity. The plague struck their first-born, the joy and hope of their families. They had slain the

white out

Plague 10:

DEATH OF THE FIRSTBORN

Son of The Sun, Aten, Born To Live and Rule Forever

Son of the God of mischief, Created To Murder The True Son and Take HIS Place

Jehovah Sends The Destroyer To Murder The Firstborn Son of God/Sa Ra/Pharaoh

✓ Destroyer comes from the etymon meaning "dove"
✓ Must See My Video: WILL THE REAL HOLY GHOST PLEASE MANIFEST

Come; let us *Read In Tongues* and have a closer look at the Scriptures with their definitions…

Exodus 11:4-7 and 12:23-24   Death of The Firstborn

And Moses said, Thus saith the LORD, About midnight will I go out into the midst of Egypt: And all the firstborn in the land of Egypt shall die, from the firstborn of Pharaoh that sitteth upon his throne, even unto the firstborn of the maidservant that is behind the mill; and all the firstborn of beasts. And there shall be a great cry throughout all the land of Egypt, such as there was none like it, nor shall be like it any more. But against any of the children of Israel (wrestle with The Creator to rule as god) shall not a dog ((Hebrew) male prostitute (English) Cynic philosopher, faultfinder) move his tongue (bind), against man (605. 'anash = desperately wicked) or beast ({"the silent dove in distant places," title of Psalm 56} H929. b@hemah = mute, from H482. 'elem = mute justice, See: H3128. yownath 'elem r@choqiymyownath, dove of (the) silence (i.e. dumb Israel) of (i.e. among) distances (i.e. strangers); the title of a ditty (used for a name of its melody):--Jonath-elem-rechokim): that ye may know how that the LORD doth put a difference between the Egyptians (Anguish; Weigh oppression) and Israel (rule God (Exodus 11:4-7)).

For the LORD will pass through to smite the Egyptians (Anguish; Weigh oppression); and when he seeth the blood upon the lintel, and on the two side posts, the LORD will pass over the door, and will not suffer the destroyer (Jonah or Jonas, a dove; he that oppresses; destroyer) to come in unto your houses to smite you. And ye shall observe this thing for an ordinance to thee and to thy sons for ever (Exodus 12:23-24).

Exodus12:41 - 42

And it came to pass at the end of the four hundred and thirty years, even the selfsame day it came to pass, that all the hosts of the LORD went out from the land of Egypt. It is a night to be much observed unto the LORD for bringing them out from the land of Egypt: this is that night of the LORD to be observed of all the children of Israel in their generations.

Captive's Log

4 April 2015 is Passover.

All over the world the image/heirs of Shem and Japheth are commemorating the day when Jehovah the God of mischief had them conjure up the greatest act of sorcery known to mankind. They slaughtered a lamb and put its blood on the doorposts of their houses so that an **Evil Spirit,** called **THE DESTROYER,** would pass over their houses; sparing their firstborn from death, all while it **slaughtered** the firstborn of **the Hamitic seed.**

Hmmm, there is that Spirit, again…the Destroyer…**THE DOVE!**

I am opening up your understanding with spiritual revelations that have the power to inflict great anguish on those who sin against yOur God. This 10th Plague: "The Death of the Firstborn" was a war between Dove and Dove…the archrival white Dove against the dark-colored bird, which is the Egyptian Falcon.

The Scripture says the firstborn Son of God was begotten by The Holy Ghost. It also says The Holy Ghost descended in bodily shape like a dove and lighted upon The Son of God and abode *(remained)* on Him. If you look back into 10,000 years' worth of history, the only lasting image that you will see having a bird upon his neck is a Pharaoh.

Captive's Log

That bird is the dark-colored bird-- the Falcon. The Falcon, not the white Dove, is the image of the real Holy Ghost.

In Plague 5, the Murrain, the camouflage message is the prophetic death of Christ. THE TEN PLAGUES OF EXODUS **are all about killing The Son of God/Pharaoh and His Holy Ghost.** Shemetic and Japhetic etymologists have just about made this knowledge disappear. I only know it because The Holy Ghost and The Lord God Alpha Khen Omega are yet teaching it to me via dreams and vision and via books that are now out of print. The Shemetic and Japhetic heirs want this knowledge about the dark-colored bird, The Holy Ghost and His Christ, To disappear, To die because it has the power To shake ones faith and To deceive one. **But, in the end, the only ones shaken and deceived shall be Shem and Japheth themselves.**

Today, for this Passover, Shem's and Japheth's and Jehovah's spells and conjurations shall not save them. The only salvation is in the blood of the living Lamb and in the testimony that He is **RIGHT NOW** giving to the Redeemed.

That testimony is that He is Pharaoh Akhenaton. He is The Aten-in-His-new name-The Lord God Alpha Khen Omega. He is alive and He is **RIGHT NOW** sealing the redeemed in their foreheads (Revelation 7:3).

All who believe shall say,

"COME, LORD GOD ALPHA KHEN OMEGA, COME!"

Page 4 of 4

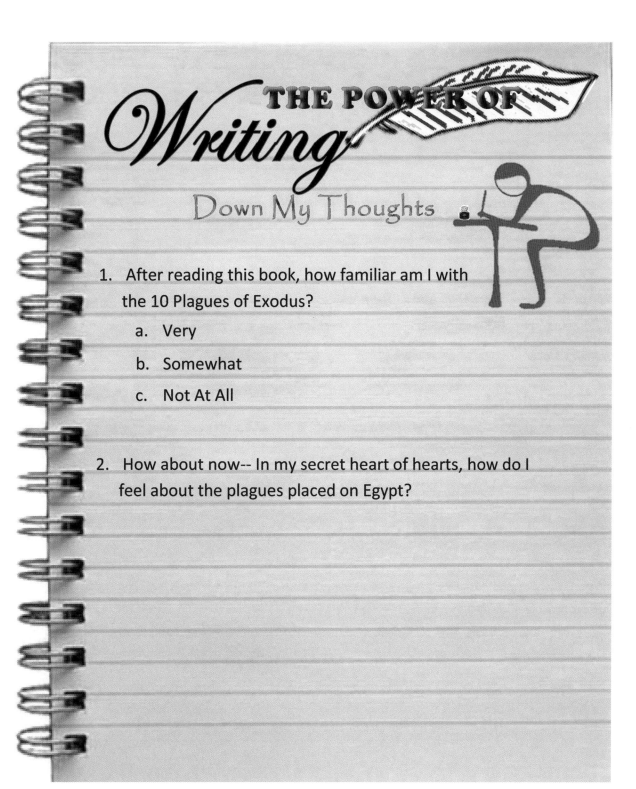

THE POWER OF Writing

Down My Thoughts

1. After reading this book, how familiar am I with the 10 Plagues of Exodus?

    a. Very

    b. Somewhat

    c. Not At All

2. How about now-- In my secret heart of hearts, how do I feel about the plagues placed on Egypt?

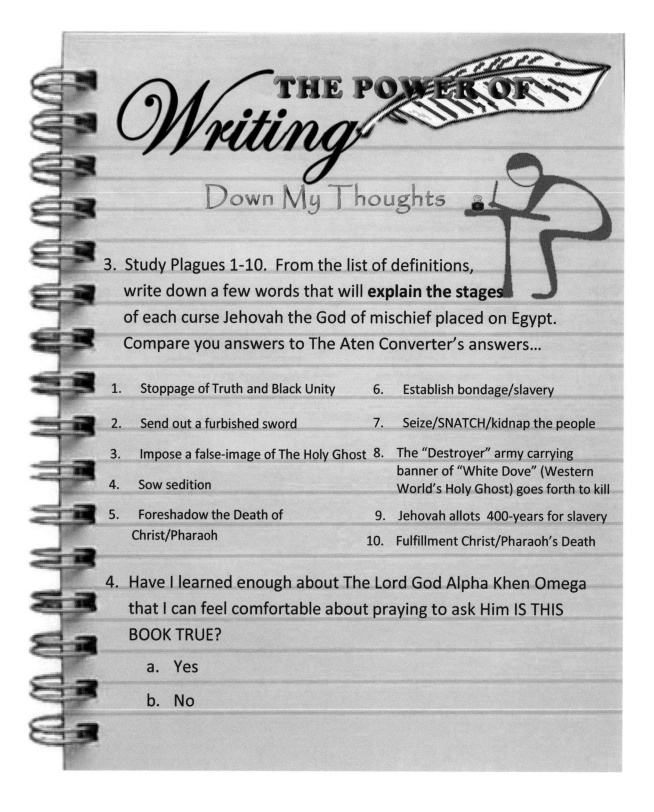

THE POWER OF Writing
Down My Thoughts

3. Study Plagues 1-10. From the list of definitions, write down a few words that will **explain the stages** of each curse Jehovah the God of mischief placed on Egypt. Compare you answers to The Aten Converter's answers...

1. Stoppage of Truth and Black Unity

2. Send out a furbished sword

3. Impose a false-image of The Holy Ghost

4. Sow sedition

5. Foreshadow the Death of Christ/Pharaoh

6. Establish bondage/slavery

7. Seize/SNATCH/kidnap the people

8. The "Destroyer" army carrying banner of "White Dove" (Western World's Holy Ghost) goes forth to kill

9. Jehovah allots 400-years for slavery

10. Fulfillment Christ/Pharaoh's Death

4. Have I learned enough about The Lord God Alpha Khen Omega that I can feel comfortable about praying to ask Him IS THIS BOOK TRUE?

    a. Yes

    b. No

Make Sure To Cross Reference With **SPIRITUAL BIPOLAR: GOD IS THE PEACE IN YOUR HEART THAT CALMS THE VOICES ABOVE YOUR HEAD.**

Page 96

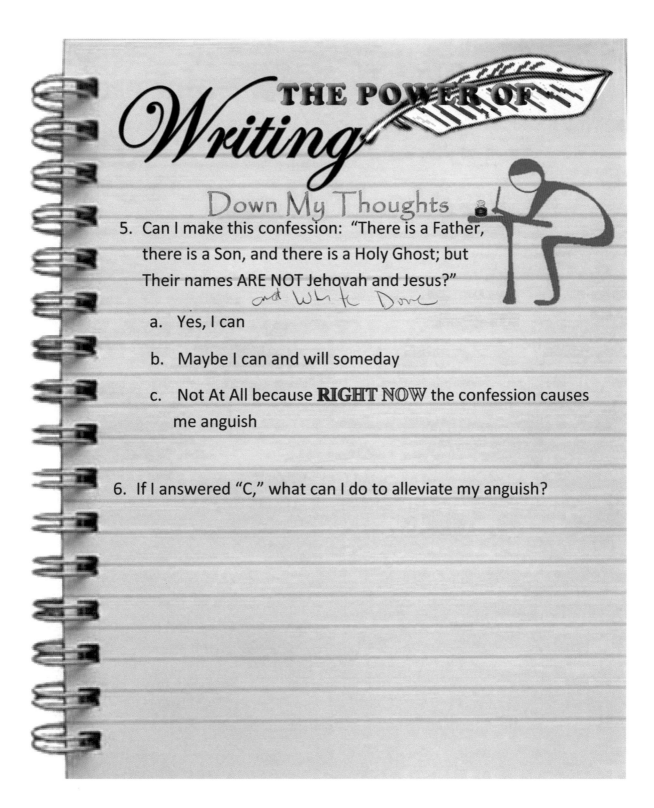

THE POWER OF *Writing*
Down My Thoughts

5. Can I make this confession: "There is a Father, there is a Son, and there is a Holy Ghost; but Their names ARE NOT Jehovah and Jesus?" *and White Dove*

   a. Yes, I can

   b. Maybe I can and will someday

   c. Not At All because **RIGHT NOW** the confession causes me anguish

6. If I answered "C," what can I do to alleviate my anguish?

Revelation 22:17

And the Spirit and the bride say, Come. And let him that heareth say, Come. And let him that is athirst come. And whosoever will, let him take the water of life freely.

Our Father said, "Verily I say unto you, Except ye BE CONVERTED, and become as little children *like us*, ye shall not enter into the kingdom of heaven (Matthew 18:3)."

Make Sure To Cross Reference With **SPIRITUAL BIPOLAR: GOD IS THE PEACE IN YOUR HEART THAT CALMS THE VOICES ABOVE YOUR HEAD.**

Page 98

Lyrics Credits:

(Page 81) "Cell Therapy." Soul Food. 7 November 1995. ⌐ₐbel

Picture Credits:

(Page 100) Gold Medalist, Tommie Smith, "Black Power Salute."

Some of the pictures and gifs within this publication were taken from:

www.google.com (I only used gifs labeled with "permission to reuse").

www.wikipedia.com

Microsoft Word's Clipart

Pencil drawings are by Cortez Sei Mantor.

Victory over the Beast, his mark, his image, and the number of his name.

Give yourself and your followers a Black Power Salute

Score
page 100

Go Tell It On The Mountain

Dogs Outside The Gates of The Holy City

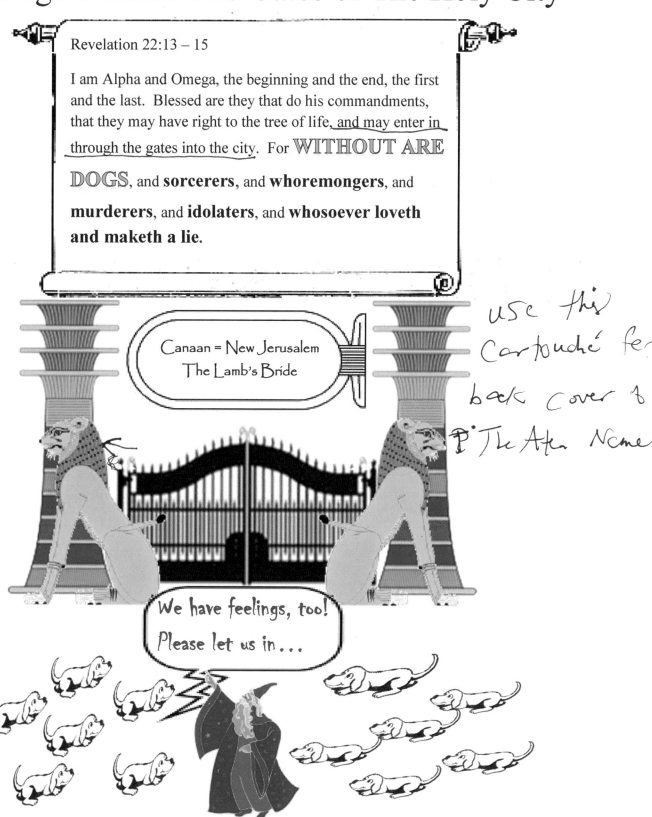

Revelation 22:13 – 15

I am Alpha and Omega, the beginning and the end, the first and the last. Blessed are they that do his commandments, that they may have right to the tree of life, and may enter in through the gates into the city. For WITHOUT ARE DOGS, and **sorcerers**, and **whoremongers**, and **murderers**, and **idolaters**, and **whosoever loveth and maketh a lie**.

Canaan = New Jerusalem
The Lamb's Bride

We have feelings, too! Please let us in . . .

Jehovah the God of mischief terrorizes Egyptians with
10 plagues that Curses Them To Death

The Completed Translation
Of Jehovah the God of mischief
~~Speaking~~ From Outside The Temple
Bullying

<u>What The Message From The 10 Plagues From Jehovah the God of mischief Really Says:</u>

Jehovah the God of mischief makes terroristic threats
in the form of 10 plagues ~~placed~~ on Egypt

Take of the River Nile that runs through the African Continent and *pour my blood into it* until

the people become ashamed, disappointed and confused. They shall become dumb until their

deaths. But I will bless you *(heirs of Shem and Japheth)* and you shall thrive. But the Egyptians

shall have no more God; nor Pharaoh, Son of God; nor King. His people shall look for Him, but

He shall not come; and they shall be confused until they develop the Confusion of Face, *which*

causes them **to wrestle** *with their own Fathers until they convert over to me, your Father.*

I, Jehovah the God of mischief, speak to those who draw out and make an excerpt of Egypt's

authoritative holy texts: Say unto your Teacher: Take a rod and stretch it out over the

Egyptian's places of intelligent hearing; upon the ears of those who weigh those of us that

cause their anguish and oppressions; make the rod interrupt their sovereignty and Black unity;

make the rod dry up all the strength of all the African divinity, even to the bones of The Ancient

of Days. Hold the rod until it causes them to be sad and to severely grieve; stay the rod of thine

hand upon the Egyptians until death and dumbness surmounts them all, and until there is a

stoppage of Truth from Maat, and until there is no longer anyone, neither of God nor Goddess,

nor male nor female, to beget pure, clean, holy boys or girls.

I, Jehovah the God of mischief, speak to those who draw out and make an excerpt of Egypt's authoritative holy texts, and who are willing to act on my behalf in the place of The Aten: Go before The Pharaoh, The Son of God, and say to Him: Leaping with joy, I bring a furbish sword against You, against your entire Continent, every country, every state and city, until I get to Your apartment, into the very bed where You sleep. And I will come upon Thee, and all Thy people, even all Thine servants.

I, Jehovah the God of mischief, speak to those who draw out to make an excerpt and write an exegesis of Egypt's authoritative holy texts: Say unto your Teacher: Stretch out the rod again and smite The Falcon that is The Holy Ghost. Make Him to die and to disappear. And I will give mine own White Dove as their Holy Spirit. Plant a vineyard and fix your eyes on the birth-bed of The Pharaoh, Son of God, and on all His people who will take it upon themselves to weigh my oppressive works that I lay upon them in the threshing floor to cause them perpetual anguish....

Then those who wake the dead and oppose The Pharaoh said to Him: This is the finger of Jehovah the God of mischief; and Jehovah said to those who write an excerpt: Appeal unto the intelligence of The Aten, The Son of God and say unto Him: I am approaching and drawing nearer to Thee with my great army. We go forth to sow sedition against You throughout the world; and wheresoever the Egyptians are mine oppressive hand shall find them to cause them anguish and to make them ashamed and disappointed in You.

Mine hand shall be upon them because I have bought them for my property *when I came upon them with my servant Joseph, whose name means "Add to me another son." I caused such a grievous famine that the Hamitic seed sold me all their resources, then their land, and finally, their very own bodies and soul into my bondage so that I would let them live and not die of the hunger.* They are my chattel. They shall be my slaves until the light of Your redemption spread out upon them. But before the Redemption, I shall murder You and destroy the anointing and subdue all the sons of God who are smart enough to the truth.

When I bring the death, I will put a difference between my servants that bedust (wrestle against) The Creator and Your sons whom I have enslaved so that they might not weigh my oppressive works; and there shall nothing die of all my servants who rule as gods.

And, I, Jehovah the God of mischief, said to those who make an excerpt of Egypt's authoritative holy texts; and to the Teacher: Blow with your breath into the air; plague all of Ham; speak words; utter spells to bring the people into the snare of captivity to fulfill the curse of bondage that Noah damned them to in order for us to enter into THE REST. From the womb, bedust The Creator God and His people to take their places and enter into their REST.

To morrow, I will capture you and train you to seize The Creator God, Re-Harakhti-in-his-name-Shu-who-is Aten and His people. We shall cause them such anguish and oppression such as has not been since the foundation of the world of Ham. We shall oppress them until they sit down together as Ham and counsel and instruct one another on how to end their oppression *(which thing they cannot do for I have stretched mine hand over their Black unity to make them recoil over their own faces)*. We shall come upon all the enslaved, even the slave in the seat of jealousy and those of the redemption; we shall come upon them until they lose their Pharaonic, Christ-ian anointing and until they die.

My great army: The White Dove...Alexander the Great (for his generation)...and Abaddon and Apollyon (for your generation) shall utterly destroy the Hamitic seed, for we are The Destroyers. We shall besiege the Throne of Pharaoh Akhenaton, The Aten, The Great Light, The Sun of righteousness, amidst the tribulation and sedition.

And when The Aten is besieged with tribulation and sedition, during his going down, I shall bring my religion upon my naked, strong thief. And, I, Jehovah the God of mischief, shall reveal myself to him in all my greatness to twist him away from The Aten and hide His light so that my naked, strong thief can officially and mentally judge the works of Gods, as it appertains to 400 years of bondage. My thief shall judge whether it be expedient for his nation to serve The Aten or me. *(And he will choose me: for I have chosen him)*. And he shall bind all peoples with my religion.

I, Jehovah the God of mischief, said unto those who draw out to make an exegesis and excerpt of Egypt's authoritative holy texts: Stretch out thine hand toward those who hear intelligently: twist them away from light, hide The Aten from all them who weigh my oppressive works; twist them away from the light three times, for three times I shall cause them to have 400 years of bondage. They shall not commune nor confer with one another to solve the issues of their bondage. They shall not even see their bondage coming, for I have blinded their eyes with thick darkness that they can always feel and fear me. But upon my children that bedust The Creator and rule as gods, I shall be to you all as a light instead of The Great Light of the Sun, and you all shall not know that I am the darkness, as well.

And he who draws out to make an excerpt of Egypt's authoritative holy texts and twists it said: Jehovah the God of mischief said: About midnight I will go out into the midst of those who shall weigh my oppressive works and all the firstborn in the land of Ham, from the firstborn of The Creator God to the first born of the Pharaoh, Son of God, to the firstborn of his maids and even the firstborn of his beast, shall die. And their cry shall be great, such as has never been before in Ham. But against the children of those who bedust The Creator to rule as gods, shall not a male prostitute, nor cynical faultfinder, speak against me nor my muted justice *system* nor against the silence of my White Dove, no matter how desperately wicked the binding: that ye may know that I, Jehovah the God of mischief, does put a difference between those who feel the afflictions of my anguish-causing bondage, and you, my children that rule as gods.

For I, Jehovah the God of mischief, will pass through to smite Ham and when I see the blood of my blessings upon your door, I will not suffer my Destroyers...my Holy Spirit in the form of a White Dove...and my army brandishing the furbished sword...to come into your houses to smite you. And ye shall observe all these ordinance to thee and thy sons for ever.

War
Of
Gog and Magog

For all this: On Sunday, 13 June 1999, Thou, O Lord God Alpha Khen Omega, declared into my hearing, "The City's at war...the city's at war...the city...the city...the city's at war."

Jehovah the God of mischief Terrorizes
the Egyptians with 10 Plagues that
Curses them Until Death or
Until They Convert Back to Their Godhead

The Completed Translation
of His Bullying From Outside
The Temple Where The
Dogs and Sorcerer Gather

Proof

Made in the USA
Charleston, SC
27 July 2015